Healing the Hurt

HEALING THE HURT

REBUILDING RELATIONSHIPS WITH YOUR CHILDREN

A SELF-HELP GUIDE FOR PARENTS IN RECOVERY

Rosalie Cruise Jesse, Ph.D.

JOHNSON INSTITUTE

Minneapolis 1990

Published by Johnson Institute
7151 Metro Blvd., Suite 250
Minneapolis, Minnesota 55439

Library of Congress Cataloging-in-Publication Data

Jesse, Rosalie Cruise.
    Healing the Hurt: Rebuilding Relationships with your Children
    A Self-Help Guide for Parents in Recovery

Includes bibliographical references.
1. Children of alcoholics—Psychology. 2. Children of narcotic
addicts—Psychology. 3. Alcoholics—Family relationships.
4. Narcotic addicts—Family relationships. 5. Parent and child.
I. Title.
HV5132.J47 1990 362.29′ 13—dc20 90-42834 CIP
ISBN 0-935908-54-4

Dedication

This book is dedicated to Dr. Vernon E. Johnson, founder of the Johnson Institute, a name that has become synonymous with the family treatment of chemical dependence.

Thanks to Dr. Johnson and his emphasis on early intervention and aftercare, recovering parents have a much greater chance of healing the hurt of their children.

Acknowledgments

My special thanks to Carole Remboldt of the Johnson Institute for having thought about this book for as many years as I have wanted to write it, for knowing that the time had come for the book to be written, and for selecting me as its author.

Loving appreciation is also extended to Carol Carson, my long-time and very dear friend, who is a wonderful source of encouragement for my writing. She reads my books and tells me that she learns from them just when I most need to hear that!

Finally, to Roger Purnelle, my husband, who shares my journey and heals my hurt and from whom I have learned the gentle art of rebuilding relationships: *Merci beaucoup pour qui tu es.*

Contents

Introduction

Recovery from chemical dependence and co-dependence can be a rewarding journey. I am exuberant when a parent begins the most difficult but exciting adventure of laying aside chemicals and starts to face life squarely. The respect I have for the parent in recovery continues to grow. As I see more and more adults trying to make life better for their children than it was for them—through the process of recovery—I want to applaud. I know that the family has begun a new course. This new direction will lead to a better way of life not only for parents and their children but also for our world.

I've never known a time when I wasn't involved in some way with families in recovery. I grew up in one. My earliest work in the mental health field was dedicated to helping children of chemically dependent parents. I've since learned that it's important to help the parent help the child. Today, as a clinical psychologist, one of the first questions parents ask me when I begin to work with them is "How can you teach us about parenting unless you've done it yourself?" This is a fair question, and I understand the basis for it. Unless one has lived with the day-to-day frustrations and sometimes bewildering experiences of being a parent, one is prone to come across with a rather lofty, ivory-tower approach to child rearing. So let me respond to these concerns: "Yes, I am a parent, and I have traveled the same path that you are traveling—all the way from the crib of my child to rebuilding a relationship during adulthood. I have learned from my successes, but I have learned more from my mistakes."

Some of my most important learning has been from the children in recovery with whom I've worked over the past twenty years. These children, together with their recovering parents, have been my teachers; they have helped shape many of the important ideas that I'll be sharing in this book.

This book stresses the need for younger children to become involved in a process of healing during their parents' recovery from chemical dependence. The book offers help on how to heal the hurt that may have been inflicted on the child. Most of the ideas are

1

applicable to rebuilding relationships with teenagers and young adults as well.

Don't look for specific "cures" for the kinds of child-rearing problems that occur daily. These problems certainly frustrate and confuse parents in recovery. But I encourage you to seek outside assistance, if necessary, at the time problems occur.

The first part of the book describes how chemical dependence harms relationships between parents and their children. This is directed primarily to recovering chemically dependent parents and codependents, but the concepts also apply equally to parents who are recovering from other forms of addictive disorders (food addiction, gambling or sexual addictions, physical or sexual abuse) and to parents who are adult children of alcoholics. In the second part of the book, the principles and guidelines for rebuilding relationships are important for all recovering parents and their children.

The important idea behind this book is that the influence of addictive behaviors in a family—even generations removed—can affect children. As we commence this part of the journey, I want to extend my congratulations and offer my support in the pages ahead. Rebuilding a relationship with your child can be difficult, challenging, but eternally rewarding!

About the Author

Rosalie Cruise Jesse, Ph.D., is a clinical psychologist in private practice. She is the Director of the Alvarado Center for Counseling and Psychology in San Diego, California. Her pioneering work with children inspires us to see as absolutely essential the healing of the parent-child relationship during recovery.

Editor's Note

We use the term "alcohol or other drugs" in this book to emphasize that alcohol *is* a drug—just like tranquilizers, cocaine, marijuana, heroin, or any other mind-altering substance. We also sometimes use the term "chemical dependence" because it covers dependence on *all* these mind-altering drugs and because it's short and simple.

Too often people talk about "alcohol *or* drugs" or "alcohol *and* drugs" as if alcohol were somehow different from drugs and in a category by itself. True, our culture, our government, even our laws treat alcohol differently from the way they treat other drugs such as pot, crack, or smack. But the symptoms of dependence are essentially the same for all these mind-altering drugs, and there is an urgent need to find ways to prevent or intervene with their use.

The usage of the pronouns *he* or *she* throughout this book was chosen for ease of readability. We never deliberately intend to sexually stereotype children or parents. In most instances, the masculine or feminine use of a pronoun is really interchangeable.

This book combines two literary forms, fiction and expository writing. The use of the fictional account of the Parents in Recovery group has been for the purpose of protecting the identity of individuals with whom Dr. Jesse has worked clinically during their recovery. If any of the characters bear resemblance to actual persons, that is only because the fictional form has been successful.

PART I

1 | The Hurt That Blinds

"I'm a single parent in recovery from alcohol and drugs. Do you know what that *means*?" The woman's voice on the phone was calm and controlled.

I thought a few moments before answering. "Being a single parent can be very demanding. Add to that the demands of recovery, and you must feel overwhelmed at times. You have my deepest respect."

There was silence at the other end of the line.

"And perhaps sometimes you start to feel guilty, wondering how your children have been hurt by chemical dependence."

"Or even *if* they've been hurt. Just before I left treatment, I picked up this book that's supposed to help me help my children. If I wasn't guilty before, I am now."

"And that's why you're calling."

"The book says that my kids are supposed to be told that I'm *sick*. So last night I sat down to try to explain that I'm 'sick.' Know what happened? The oldest turned around and walked out of the room. The boy started banging on his drum so loudly I was ready to scream. And the youngest girl started to cry."

"How old are your children?"

"Five, nine, and thirteen."

"I can see how the word *sick* could disturb your child, especially the two youngest. At those ages children are particularly concrete in their logic. When they hear that a parent is sick, they can become quite fearful and overburdened, even though they may not express these feelings with words."

"Tell me about it! This morning my little girl was crying again, and she asked me if I was going to die. I'm the *only* parent she has, and now I feel guilty for worrying her. She's been through enough already."

"I can understand your reasoning."

"So, no more books by people who've probably never been in my situation! Or never even had kids. I need to hear from other *parents in recovery*."

The woman assured me that she was actively involved in an aftercare program as well as in a twelve-step network. "But I need to talk to someone about being a parent in recovery," she re-emphasized. "Sometimes I feel like I'm really losing it, and those times usually have something to do with my kids. If it was just me, recovery would be a breeze. But I've got me, a career, and three children to deal with every single day."

"Have you tried talking about this at your meetings?"

"Yeah, just the other night. Some wise guy pipes up and says, 'So give up your career and stop complaining. Stay home and take care of your kids like a mother is supposed to do.'"

"You must have felt very discounted."

"To hear a 'give up' message? I've had to fight my way through life to get where I am, and here this clown is telling me to give it all up. I might as well go back to drinking!"

"Do you have a sponsor?"

"Yes, God bless her, but she keeps telling me 'not to worry' or that I'm doing 'the best I can.' The lady has a wealth of practical information about how to stay sober, but she doesn't know much about kids. That's why I'm calling you—someone who specializes in kids *and* recovery."

"But you're also looking for others with whom to share. I can imagine that being a single parent must be very lonely when you need to talk about problems with your children. Perhaps you'd like to be part of a parents in recovery group?"

"Yeah, that's what I'd like. Do you have such a group?"

"Not yet."

"Well, let's start one. I can think of a couple of other people who'd probably want to come. How many do we need?"

"Six would be ideal."

"OK, there's this guy, Fred, from one of my meetings. He came up to me the other night and confided that he doesn't know the first thing about how to help his kids either. I'll ask him to bring his wife, too. And another single parent, Chuck, is beside himself about the problems he's caused his kids. Do you know of anyone else?"

Actually I'd just been contacted by a couple who'd been court-referred to me for counseling. Their son had been living in foster care for several months because of the parent's heavy involvement with drugs. Now in recovery, they were about to reunify as a family, and they were eager to learn a new and better way of parenting.

"So that's our six!" The woman on the phone exulted. "We can talk about our problems as parents, and then we can get your input about how to help our children. I'm open to anything except dwelling on 'sickness.'"

"Then, how about 'wellness'?" I suggested.

"That's it. A wellness model—something about *healing*."

"I'll give it some thought."

"You do that, and when you decide *what* needs to be healed, give me a call. My name's Karra." She gave me her business and home phone numbers, and then continued quickly, "I'm going to hand-letter some announcements for our group. I'm a whiz at calligraphy—at least I used to be before I was so heavily into chemicals. Seems then I stopped doing everything except work and drink and use. My kids got less and less of my time. At first I could see they were hurting. Then, funny thing, it was like I was blind. I didn't know if they were hurting; I was so oblivious. And too caught up in my own hurt to *see* theirs."

"You've just answered your own question about what needs to be healed. Our group can concentrate on healing the *hurt*."

Parents in Recovery

We can learn a lot about the hurt of our children when we are able to listen to each other as *parents in recovery*. Let's tune in now to one such group where parents have come together to support each other in extending recovery to their children. Guiding the meeting, I have announced my belief that parents are the most effective healers of a child's hurt—even when a parent inflicted that hurt.

Tonight the group has agreed to let down their barriers and to share their innermost conflicts about being a parent in recovery. Regardless of how silly or how negative they might sound, the participants know that they will hear no judgment or condemnation from the other group members. I encourage honest reactions.

"Honesty is the *only* policy," the group agreed. "By learning to face the truth about ourselves, we'll help our children."

"OK," Fred resolved, "I'll start. *I'm ashamed to say it but sometimes I don't think I can stay with my family and stay sober.*" He looked down to avoid the eyes of the other group members but especially the stunned expression of Mimi, his wife.

"I know what you mean." Karra came to Fred's rescue. "I used to think my kids were driving me to drink. Now I think they're driving me crazy."

"But how could you think of leaving them?" Mimi said to Karra. Everyone knew that her question was really for Fred.

"Oh, I'd never leave them," Karra explained. "I'm a *single parent*."

"You make that sound like a prison term—a life sentence," Chuck said.

"Definitely no time off for good behavior," Karra replied. "Guess that doesn't apply to you, Chuck. Sorry!"

Chuck was the other single parent in the group. His best recovery efforts had not convinced his wife that he had really changed. Punitively, she had insisted on a separation, forcing him to move out of their family home. He rarely had visitation with his five children. His family didn't even acknowledge his "good behavior."

"Just be grateful, man!" Sam said. "Your kids didn't have to see you all messed up, coming off the stuff, ya' know? Like, maybe they needed time off from you. Get it?"

"You sound like my wife."

"Take a good look at Sam and me," Sara said. "We learned big time about kids needing time off. Back when we were living on the streets, the cops took one look at our boy, Seth, and whamo! Seth was off to this foster home. They wouldn't even let us visit him 'til we cleaned up our act."

"We freaked out," Sam said. "So we started jumping through hoops to get the kid back. Still do. Whatever the social worker says, we do it. We know Seth is gonna have his little hang-ups a long time."

"Like, he was hurt big time, by *our drinking and using*," Sara said.

Sam and Sara were intense about recovery. (Their previous destructive use of alcohol and street drugs led to family disintegration. They lost everything to chemicals. In the end, they literally lived on the streets, selling drugs. Court intervention with their son had finally convinced them to begin treatment.) Now Sam and Sara were an inspiration to the group.

"The truth is," Fred said, "I don't know *how* to be a father. Maybe that sounds odd, but who taught me? *My dad*. And he was a *drunk*. I learned how to be a drunk. Not a father. I said *I'd never do to my kids what he did to me*—I'd leave first."

Mimi's expression softened. She, too, had grown up with an abusive, alcoholic parent. She still suffered nameless fears and sometimes panic attacks because of her core fear of abandonment. She had listened to Fred's earlier comment about leaving as a terrible threat. Now, listening to him share his childhood, she was empathic with his hurt.

"I don't *really* know how to be a parent either," Mimi confessed. "I bluff. I try to look good. I exhaust myself trying to prove I'm not like my alcoholic mother. That's why I've never touched a drop of liquor. But I've got my own little problems. And, just out of sheer blindness—denial—I've hurt my kids in a different sort of way."

"Try single parenting *and* recovery," Karra said. "Plus a career. Plus being a taxi service for kids. Twelve-step meetings every few days. And now *these* meetings. I mean, are you kidding me, or what? Who has *time* to see all this hurt?"

The struggle that I heard from these parents was familiar: *How do we go about healing the hurt of our children when we are still struggling with our own recovery?*

The six members of this group had affected the lives of fifteen children below the age of eighteen. I knew that each parent suffered guilt, confusion, and hurt. They hurt for their children who had suffered a premature disillusionment with life. Who could ever make up for that?

The Hurt That Blinds

Who of us doesn't know something about childhood hurt? From our own experiences as children, many of us learned what NOT to do as parents. We didn't want to repeat our parents' mistakes with our own sons and daughters. So we vowed to do better by our children than had been done to us. We pledged to be the best parents in the world.

Then something happened. Chemical dependence began to infiltrate family life. At first the troubled family patterns were subtle, and we could hardly see them. As problems became more blatant, we may have been like Karra, blind to what was happening around us. We even lost sight of that earlier commitment to our children and began to repeat with them scenes from our own childhood. Despite our best intentions, *we were doing to our children what had been done to us—causing them hurt.*

Denial: The Great Cover-up

Denial both accounts for the hurt that we cause our children and limits our ability to *see* their hurt. Once upon a time as children, we had free access to our hurt. We could *see* the horrors of our parents' chemical dependence. But then during the teen years and young adulthood, we erected psychological defenses as barriers to prevent the experience of childhood hurt.

A primary defense of persons affected by chemical dependence is *denial*. We don't know that we're using denial, because our choice of this defense is largely unconscious. If we can make a conscious decision to distort information when we *know* the truth, this is not denial. Rather, it is a deliberate distortion. This is a lie or falsehood. For example, a wife may say to her husband who has just finished a six-pack of beer: "You've had too much to drink!"

Her husband replies, "Whadaya mean too much to drink? I've just had *one* beer!" The husband may be *in denial* about the extent of his drinking problem, but he has deliberately chosen to *lie* about how much he has had to drink. When we can perceive accurately but choose to distort the truth, we have chosen to lie.

The type of denial that we see in chemically dependent persons is part of the disease process of addiction. Psychological denial actually has been strengthened by chemicals. Alcohol, other drugs, and even food, when used in excess, serve as anesthetics; they numb painful emotional states. Until the chemicals are removed, the person may not be able to do anything other than deny. He or she is said to be living *in denial*.

Denial and Self-Centered Parenting

More years ago than I'd care to remember, I learned a lot of high-school Latin, now mostly forgotten except for one phrase:

Ego amo te. (*I* love you.)

Ego is the Latin word for "I." In this book, I will be using the word *ego* to talk about *the psychological part of us that filters the messages of this "I" whose purpose is to protect the self-image.* The ego does this by blocking negative messages and exaggerating positive ones.

Before chemical use began, the self-image for many of us from chemically dependent families was actually quite negative. But under the influence of the chemical, the ego swells like a hot air balloon, filling us with grandiose ideas. We begin to feel euphoric and invulnerable. We refuse to admit to weaknesses or limitations. We deny the hurt that we may be causing others and concentrate on how they're hurting us. If a problem exists in our relationships with our children, it is because *they* (or a spouse, or an ex-spouse, or some other person of blame) are at fault.

We don't realize that we are actually being imprisoned by the ego. Even in recovery, the ego can drive us to feel all important, all powerful, and perfect. But we're always afraid of being found out as wrong, or stupid, or even cruel. So we have a difficult time relaxing, letting down, and being genuine. Compulsively, we start to over compensate by working hard or being fastidious and exacting. Unable to accept our own imperfections, we certainly don't want to accept those of our children. We tend to see their problems or their hurt as a moral indictment against our imperfect parenting. We have lost the ability to step out of our own self-centered frame of reference.

Because of our perfectionism, we have difficulty seeing the world through the eyes of a child. The childishness of our sons and daughters can baffle us. We certainly don't want to admit that parenting in recovery overwhelms, annoys, frustrates, and confuses us or that we sometimes feel totally inept.

Now can you see the important question that is before us? *How do adults in recovery who sometimes feel small, childlike, and helpless suddenly begin to heal the hurt of their children?* Stripped of power and poise, how can we do anything other than concentrate on our own need for healing?

Beyond the gateway to recovery lies the journey. We may be tempted to enter the gate alone, leaving behind other family members, especially our children. We're too *afraid* to face the truth about inflicting hurt on our children in the way that we said we'd never do.

But on this particular journey called recovery, we won't make it very far down the road until we begin to receive messages of hurt from the children we have left behind. These messages will usually show up in a disguised form such as problem behavior, physical complaints, or school conflicts, just to name a few, that can threaten our own recovery.

2 | Messages of Hurt

"I'm not sure that my children were even hurt by my drinking." Karra looked around the group to test each member's reaction to her comment.

"What makes your drinking so different from ours?" Chuck asked.

"Unlike some of you who lost everything to chemical dependence, I never lost a job. I gave my kids a beautiful home in the best neighborhood. Nice clothes. Good schools. The best in childcare. They didn't want for anything."

"Except a relationship with *you!*" Sara said.

"Are you suggesting that I was an absentee mother? Sorry to disappoint you, but I did most of my using at home when the kids were asleep."

"So, you were *there*. But you weren't *really* there," Sara continued.

"Ouch! That hurt."

Sam rushed in to protect Sara. "Hey, you struck the first blow. Maybe you didn't know it. I'll give you the benefit of the doubt. But, yeah, Sara and me lost everything to booze and other drugs. Even some kids. Now *that* really hurts. But recovery means we have to face up to the hurt we feel and the hurt we caused our kids."

"I could've sworn I just heard you say that you lost 'some kids,'" Fred said, "but I thought you and Sara had only the one boy—Seth."

"Yo, Fred, you're not tripping out. Sara and me have one kid. But I lost a couple of others somewhere along the way because of dope. It's not fun talking about it so I won't, and today there's nothing I can do about it, except hurt. And that I do. More than you know. Who likes to think they hurt their own flesh and blood by being strung out on chemicals?"

"We're all in the same boat," Fred said. "It doesn't matter how much money we have, it won't heal hurt."

"Back to Karra," Mimi said. "We can't leave her hanging. Let's hear more about your children, Karra."

"OK, the youngest is Sandy. She's five and a beautiful little strawberry blonde."

"Just like her mom!" Sara offered in a peacemaking gesture.

Karra smiled. "Yeah, Sandy's like me in more ways than one. Spoiled. Needs special treatment. But she's my divorce baby, so I think it's OK to pamper her."

"What's a divorce baby?" Fred asked.

"A baby that gets the divorce rolling. My ex and I were partners in a real estate company until he became threatened by my success. The jerk accused me of trying to take over the business. I was. His solution was to get me pregnant and then start a fling with our office receptionist. He dumped me for her just before Sandy was born."

"You must have been very hurt," Mimi said.

"Try humiliated. I could hear the whispering and the snickering from our employees. So I needed power. Big time! I'd already found booze; I just needed *more*. Then I found cocaine. Did that ever make me feel powerful! Finally, I was using a little marijuana in between, just to keep mellow. Then I could act like nothing bothered me. I was my usual powerful self. I plotted and schemed, and before long I was able to buy him out of the business."

"You expect us to believe your kids weren't hurt?" Chuck asked.

"I protected them!" Karra snapped. "If they were hurt, it was probably more by the divorce than by my using and boozing. Anyhow, I didn't come here to take that little guilt trip down memory lane."

"Sorry," Chuck said. "So, why'd you get sober if you had so much power?"

"After a while I couldn't manage my business. When I got so I couldn't function at home, I could always leave the kids with the maid. But the business was my sole responsibility. I saw it slipping through my fingers. I couldn't let that happen. It was my life. So I got myself to this wonderful treatment center out in the desert. I could unburden myself of all responsibilities for a whole month. Then, back to reality. Back to the kids. Back to business. Sober, I'm a whiz at real estate. But being a single parent in recovery is the hardest job I've ever had."

"With only one little girl?" Chuck asked.

"I'm working up to the other two—if you'll stop butting in. My problem child is Billy. He's nine and a regular little bully. Always in trouble at school. Demanding attention in all the wrong ways. Fighting on the playground. You name it, he does it. Constant arguing and fighting at home with his sisters, especially little Sandy. I think he really hates his sister."

"We have a son with similar problems," Mimi said. "He's almost eight. Sometimes I'm ready to blame his problems on Fred's alcoholism, but then I see a lot of my fourth grade boys acting the same way, so I say, 'No, it's just his age.'"

"Age, shmage. My Bill's just like his dad, a regular chip off the old block. That's his problem."

"Mimi's not altogether wrong," I explained. "Boys from chemically dependent families who are in the seven- to nine-year age group do show a lot of behavior problems. Both at home and at school."

"Well, what about the age thirteen?" Karra asked. "Should I be superstitious? My thirteen-year-old, Angel, is turning into a regular little witch."

"Thirteen is a difficult transition period for all children," I continued, "but it's especially turbulent for children from chemically dependent families. Deep inside, Angel may have been carrying problems all along that are just starting to erupt like a volcano. You think it's all happened overnight. But it's been building up for years."

"I named her Angel because she might as well have worn a halo. Even when I was drinking, she was the best little kid. I used to call her my straight-A child. *A* for Angel; *A* for April, the month of her birthday; and *A* for always being on the honor roll in school. Angel made me proud. Then, overnight, she turned on me."

"After you sobered up, she started to change," Mimi said. "I know. I had the same problem with our girls once Fred began his recovery."

"Angel's developing another problem that's got me worried." Karra confided this in a half-whisper as she looked around as though someone might be in the back of the room to overhear. "It's an eating problem. I mean she doesn't have any problem eating. She over eats. Binges. Hoards food and hides it. Nasty junk food. Here our cupboards are overflowing, and the housekeeper's a wonderful cook; and I've got this porky little thirteen-year-old girl sneaking food and hiding it out in her room. The place is a pig sty. When you open the door to Angel's room, the stench hits you in the face."

Sara moved nervously to the edge of her chair, speaking in a rapid-fire manner. "Yeah, like our boy Seth's got his little eating hang-ups, too, picking at his food like a little bird. At mealtime, he won't eat more than a bite or two, but I see him sneaking food into his pockets. It could be only a little pocketful of crumbs, but the kid won't leave the table until he's got his little stash of food. I catch him in the act and call him on it, but he just stares at me like I'm crazy. I don't know what to make of it, but he scares me; he's such a wiry little guy."

Sam reached out to hold Sara's hand. "Listen to me, Babe, and don't think I'm getting on your case. But Seth's been talking to me about this food thing. Like he gets real bad vibes when you push him to clean his plate. I think he feels guilty, like he's doing something wrong. Bet you don't remember what you taught Seth when you were living on the streets, 'cause you were loaded. But you'd lecture him every time you got some food—'Save some for later. Save some for later.' You told him you didn't know where our next meal was coming from, and he'd have to cooperate by saving something in his pockets— just in case. Remember? The kid's mind got warped about food. Now, all of a sudden, you're switching messages—'Clean your plate. Clean your plate.' It's blowing his mind."

Sara began to rock back and forth, her arms tightly holding her abdomen. "I don't remember—just little flashbacks. I feel so bad for Seth, how I've confused him. Who knows what other crazy stuff I taught him when I was all strung out?"

"We all did that, Sara," Chuck reached over and touched her shoulder. "God knows what I taught my kids when I was drinking. But we're in here to change things for the better now."

"One thing for sure, we can't expect our kids to switch to a brand new type of program overnight. They learned bad habits from us. I know Seth is going to have to get better gradually, just like us. He's not some little robot that you can reprogram by flipping a switch."

"So when I expect Billy to stop being a bully or Angel to act the way I think she should, I'm being unrealistic?"

"Yo!" Sam said.

"What if it's not the alcoholic parent that's making problems for the kids?" Chuck asked.

"Now that's what I was trying to say, and you jumped on me," Karra said.

"Just hear me out. We adopted this six-year-old boy. He had trouble going to sleep at night, so my wife would bring him into our bed. I argued, 'No kid should be sleeping with a man and his wife.' But

19

by the end of my drinking, my wife was using the boy's sleeping problem to move *me* out to the couch. 'You're a grown man. You can sleep by yourself,' she'd say. Seems to me, she made that boy's sleeping problems get *worse* on purpose."

"Sounds like your *wife* needs this group. I'll send her an engraved invitation," Karra said. "Now I've always let little Sandy sleep with me from the time she was born, but it's different because I don't have a husband."

"Does she have nightmares?" Mimi asked.

"Billy is the one with nightmares. Or so he says. I've always thought he's been faking it, trying to steal me away from Sandy. But frankly, I'm getting weary of talking about all these *problems*. Eating problems, sleeping problems, school problems, brothers and sisters who hate each other, and I'll bet you could go on and on and add to the list. What does it all mean? What does it have to do with *our* recovery? What does it have to do with *their* hurt?"

Hurt Is a Silent Message

When children send out their messages of hurt, they do not use words. They do not say that you have bewildered them or confused them or that they are afraid of you. Sometimes a child may say "You hurt my feelings." But even this is rare in families affected by chemical dependence.

Some children, such as Billy, send out messages of hurt through troubled behavior. Others, such as Angel, scarcely call attention to the deep hurt they are feeling because they are so busy hiding behind people-pleasing gestures. Such a child will do anything to win your approval and make you feel proud of her. She will sacrifice her very selfhood. These eager-to-please children are more concerned about meeting our needs and making us feel pleased than they are with their own accomplishments. Eventually, this child starts to feel resentful. As she struggles to gain selfhood, she may become completely negative. Her pleasure now comes from doing the *opposite* of what you expect of her. This is how she begins to realize some sense of identity that is separate from yours.

Other children, such as little Sandy, will express hurt through whiny demands. This is the child you tried to pamper as a way of relieving guilt. Perhaps she is a divorce baby or a child who was exposed to the day-to-day crises of chemical dependence. You didn't want her to hurt, so you started a pattern of fulfilling her every demand. She came to sense that you "owe her." She may not completely understand this, but she reads the silent message of *your hurt* that says you failed her. As you continue to pay, you feel as though you can never do enough, give enough, or be enough. But you continue to try. Irrationally, you fear that this child's very survival depends on you.

The Stress Factor

We know about stress. Stress is the opposite of serenity. Stress is anxiety, tension, and fear. Stress is pressure. Stress is being overwhelmed with life and feeling that you can't cope any longer. Stress is rapid heart beat, shortness of breath, weariness, headache, a knot in the pit of your stomach, and tossing and turning all night.

When parents are drinking and using, children live in family environments of severe, chronic stress. Daily parenting responsibilities start to become overwhelming. You may have helped to develop a "parentified" child as a caretaker for the entire family. These children often have to carry on without you. Even if a parent is able to provide the best of childcare (as did Karra), children still absorb that parent's tension and anxiety.

When life became unmanageable, your children experienced turmoil. You may have contributed excessive amounts of stress to their lives, often without realizing it. Sometimes you may have pushed your children beyond their coping abilities. A child may have had to care for brothers and sisters, attend school, prepare meals, and do homework. You may have exposed this child to your rantings or ravings while you or your spouse were under the influence. Or, the child may have been awake all night, holding her breath until you staggered home the next morning. When this child has to attend school later that day, she will sit lethargic and exhausted in the classroom. Life is already overwhelming her—even at her young age.

Stress in Recovery

We may not be surprised to hear that children live through high levels of stress when parents are drinking and using, but stress is also present in recovery.

Recovery implies a new way of life for the family. Any lifestyle change demands considerable adjustments on the part of the individual family members, as well as a reshuffling of family rituals, routines, and role relationships. Your children will tend to resist these changes.

The new stress of recovery is added to the reservoir of stress that your children may have been accumulating all through your drinking and using. When children resist change, they are trying to shield themselves from the burden of more stress. They may not want their parent to resume drinking and using, but they do want things to stay the same—the same rituals, routines, and rules. Particularly, when a child has been in charge of certain areas of family life, that child is not going to want to give up control automatically. The familiar is reassuring; the unknown of recovery is stressful.

Problems in Self-Regulation

Overwhelming stress can render children so emotionally numb that they may lose touch with their own bodily signals. The result is a disturbance in the capacity to regulate basic self-care functions.

Self-regulation problems also arise from a disturbed parent-child relationship. When you are first coming off a drug, you may not be very sensitive to your own self-care functions. Problems in self-monitoring are a part of the disorder of chemical dependence. If you don't take very good care of yourself, your children stand on the sidelines, watching and learning. They may pick up your worst habit patterns. They learn to ignore their own inner signals. This leads them to experience problems in self-monitoring. Difficulties in eating, sleeping, rest, hygiene, and elimination are some of the self-regulation problems that are common in children from chemically dependent families.

Problems in Self-Soothing

Children from chemically dependent families have major problems in what is known as "self-soothing" abilities. This means that your children may not have developed the inner resources to calm themselves in the face of severe stress or intense emotions.

When children lack this inner ability to self-soothe, they can't use their environment or their inner world effectively. One child may be unable to play alone with toys. Another child's agitation prevents him from using the normal childhood resources of fantasy and make-believe. Your children may become even more angry, frightened, or overwhelmed as these normal emotions continue to escalate.

Certain youngsters will even show such restlessness as a result of stress that they may be thought to have a chemical imbalance. Physicians, educators, or other professional helpers may incorrectly label a child as "hyperactive" or attention deficit disordered (ADD) when the child is merely signaling about his stress-filled life.

Problems in self-soothing show up in the classroom when the child is fidgety, restless, and talkative. The child who has grown up in a chemically dependent family experiences the normal stresses of attending school as unsettling.

At home you may lash out at your child, "What's *wrong* with you that you can't play in your room with your toys? Why do you keep pestering me?" The child receives the message that he is somehow defective, but of course, he doesn't know why.

Children with self-soothing deficits also express their emotional conflicts through bodily aches and pains. A child who is actually struggling to calm herself because she "doesn't feel well" may often excuse herself from the classroom to go to the school nurse. Her inner distress has been transformed into vague physical pain, such as a headache or a stomachache. These symptoms are the child's way of trying to handle the demands of the classroom when life in the family overwhelms her.

Symptoms also can reveal a child's basic insecurity about life. But children usually cannot tell us that they are expressing their inner hurt indirectly through obsessions, worries, fears, withdrawal, or physical complaints.

Your child's inability to self-soothe may be related to the exposure to chronic stress—as well as to disturbances in the parent-child relationship. To provide soothing to a child, you must offer a calm, serene disposition. From earliest infancy, the child requires the parent to serve as a buffer. By cooing, singing, holding, rocking, or speaking soft words of reassurance, you can shield your child from overwhelming stress. Your child will absorb these soothing functions, which later form the basis of her own ability to self-soothe.

Under the control of chemicals, you lacked sensitivity to your child's wordless signals of need. Remember, chemicals dull the senses, interfering with the largely intuitive realm of parent-child relating. You may have ignored your child when he was hungry, given a bottle when companionship was really needed, or kept the child awake when she was tired and weary. You may even have struck a child who was in distress.

As your child continues to grow and develop, he fails to acquire the inner resources for self-soothing. Many of the problems in self-regulation are associated with this inability to self-soothe. Problems of eating and sleeping, for example, are simply echoes of a child's inner need or distress.

How can your children talk to you about their problems in self-soothing? How can they put into words that they do not have the capacity to calm or comfort themselves? They cannot. Thus it is important to keep in mind that your child's symptom or behavior problem is actually a message of hurt.

When stress overwhelms and children cannot self-soothe, they may express distress through obsessions, worries, or fears that occur singly or together. An extreme fear that is expressed in a disguised form is called a phobia. Phobic symptoms are often present in such children who may fear spiders or other insects, weather conditions, certain people, and even school.

Other children who cannot self-soothe may seem numb and apathetic. As a way of trying to cope, this child has had to shut-down in the face of overwhelming stress. Already on emotional "overload," the child withdraws into daydreams or fantasy and may have difficulty completing chores or homework assignments.

Social Relationships

Children naturally love to be with other people, particularly their own age-mates. But children from chemically dependent families experience tension and conflict in social relationships. Even if a child is otherwise problem-free, he or she usually encounters difficulty getting along with others.

You may see the strained and bitter sibling relationships in your own family. Like Fred, you may feel at times that you can't live with the constant bickering and fighting and remain sober. At other times you tend to rationalize that things aren't *that* bad. You contend that even in the best of homes brothers and sisters argue and fight. To an extent this is true. You may not completely understand the nature of the resentments that your children have against each other. You may underestimate the severity of their sibling abuse, both physical and sexual. But research shows that children from chemically dependent families seem to experience more intense disharmony than do children whose parents are not chemically dependent.[1] "The secret war of siblings" is my description of these problems common to brothers and sisters in chemically dependent families.[1]

When you were drinking and using, your children may have had to band together in order to survive. Whatever emotional support they received had to come from each other. You weren't available to them. But when you try to resume leadership of the family during recovery, your children start to disband. They no longer need each other. Resentments, which may have been building all along, burst into open hostility.[2]

Peer relationships also may be awkward and inappropriate. Your children may demand to be the center of attention. Bossiness, manipulation, rivalry, and outright aggression are other ways that they may interact with peers and end up frustrated and lonely.

When Do Parents Receive Messages of Hurt?

We can't travel very far down the road of recovery until we begin to receive messages of hurt from our children. Our children will not use words to communicate. Their messages will be through symptoms or problem behavior that will make our own recovery more stressful. When we turn our attention from our program to cope with the problems of our children, we start to feel resentful: "Why isn't this child getting better instead of worse? He doesn't appreciate all the hard work of my recovery! He's driving me to drink."

When a parent becomes abstinent, why don't children's problems improve automatically? Why do they seem to get worse?

There are a couple of reasons to explain this. First, abstinence improves your ability to *see* a child's problems that may have been there all along. Now, with continued recovery, the child is beginning to feel that you're finally strong enough to cope with his problems.

Second, before you began recovery, your children had adapted to a way of life that was meant to sustain them. You may have surrendered your parenting to one or more of the children who learned to carry on without you or in spite of you. But recovery brings family reorganization. Your children may be less than thrilled as you launch this new way of life. On the one hand, they're glad that you stopped using chemicals, but they haven't learned to trust you to parent them.

Your family members seem to want to continue to function by the same rules of dysfunction that were operating before you began recovery. Your children actively resist change and new role options.

You think change will be welcomed, but you may encounter tremendous resistance from your loved ones. For example, you may want to encourage your parentified child to play more and stop bossing the other children. Your shocked when she's insulted.

What did you do wrong? Why does she accuse you of being controlling and manipulative? Why doesn't she want to be more childlike? This child will not move out of her familiar place in the family just because you say so. Your efforts are resented. Why? *Because you have failed to see her hurt.*

3 | The Hurt That Binds

"Let me be the first to admit that I've caused problems for my kids—because of my chemical dependence," Karra announced at the opening of the next group meeting.

The members broke into laughter, but Karra couldn't join in. She didn't even realize that the shift in her perception had taken place. The previous group session had moved her from denial to *awareness*.

Karra's new intellectual understanding of her children's problems was the important first step in healing their hurt. But Karra was only halfway there. Her expression tensed. "The *problem* is I'm just sick and tired of talking about all these *problems*."

Everyone in the group remained silent, waiting.

"Is it *my* fault that Angel has turned into a little witch? Or, that Billy wants to be a bully? Sure, my kids have problems. But now that I'm sober, *I'm going to change them*."

"Oh, come off it, Karra!" Chuck said. "Your kids aren't little robots. Angel isn't a witch, and Billy is probably crying out for help the only way he knows how. Remember? Those messages of hurt?"

"Yeah, don't start pushing their change-buttons yet. Not before you've listened to their hurt," Fred cautioned. "When Mimi started trying to 'fix' our kids, it backfired."

"I have no idea what you're talking about," Karra said. "But I hear your disguised criticism, gentlemen! So, please, I'd rather hear from the *mothers* in the group."

"Karra, I'm so sorry," Mimi apologized. "Fred and Chuck didn't mean to criticize. They wanted you to think about the hurt behind each child's *family role*."

"Hey, don't talk *for* me!" Chuck admonished. "I happen to agree with you that Karra's on a roll—ready to push those change-buttons—but what's a *family roll*?"

"R-o-l-e," Mimi spelled out politely. "A family role. Like a role in a play where Billy's acting out the part of a bully, and I guess you'd say Angel is starring as a witch."

"We learned about all these family roles when we went through treatment," Fred explained for Chuck's benefit.

"Hey, I got sober in a twelve-step program," Chuck said. "I still go to several meetings a week, but we don't talk about *roles*. We talk about our *selves*."

"God bless twelve-step meetings!" Sara said.

"Sara and I are also in this rap group for recovering addicts. Some of the people are right off the streets, like we used to be. Some don't even live in a family anymore. So what do they care about family roles? They make it right with their kids by drug testing and jumping through the hoops of the system. They do it because they *love* their kids. Maybe they've hurt 'em, but they still love 'em. Isn't that what's important? That our kids know we love 'em, no matter what?" Sam's passionate question seemed to stun the group.

Mimi turned to me with a desperate, please-help expression.

Then Karra asked sarcastically, "Just so the rest of us won't flunk Recovery 101, why don't you enlighten us about these *family roles*?"

Family Roles

We know that in every family certain roles develop naturally, such as those that come with the special position of being a mother or a father. A parent's role usually has something to do with the expectations of the culture about how parents take care of their young. But these parental role behaviors can and do vary greatly, even within the same culture.

I asked the group members to think for a few minutes as they tried to define what being a *mother* and a *father* means. Then I had them jot down their ideas on what being a "good" mother and a "bad" mother means. I asked them to identify what they would be *doing* if they were carrying out *role behaviors* of these good and bad mother images. Then, I asked them to do the same exercise with the "good" and "bad" father roles.

When I instructed the group to discuss where they had learned these role behaviors, most members agreed that many of their inner images of "good" and "bad" parent roles actually originated with their own experiences in childhood. Frequently, the "good" parent roles were a child's-eye view of the way their parents *should* have behaved.

If our childhood was spent in a family troubled by chemical dependence, we may have seen very dramatic role models of ineffective parenting. *These were our very own parents.* We rejected our parents as the wrong type of mom or dad. We vowed that we would never do to our children what was being done to us. But through the process of childhood learning, we could not help but absorb some of that negative information about dysfunctional parenting.

Many of us also made an effort to look about in our world to try to find other "good" parent role models. If we were lucky enough, we may have had other adult relatives who were "good" parent role models. Or, perhaps we saw the parents of our friends who lived in more functional families. But most of us who grew up in troubled homes spent a lot of time alone. Our learning may have come from books, such as fables, fairy tales, or adventure and romance novels.

More than likely we also turned to our favorite home companion, the television set. The television served as a kind of substitute parent, which offered comfort, soothing, learning, and the promise of a better way of life. We became so absorbed in the promises of television that we never stopped to question whether or not they were attainable. We believed in fantasy. This provided relief from the pathetic melodrama of our own family struggle. We learned how "good" parents interact with their children from any one of a number of TV sitcoms. These television families seemed perfectly compatible with our innocent, but childish need to see life with a happy ending.

Chemical Dependence and Family Roles

Chemically dependent family systems are complex and chaotic. But chaos is bewildering. So, living within these systems, we can become confused and disoriented. Then we look for ways to make sense out of the confusion. We naturally tend to want to simplify.

One way that mental health professionals try to simplify their understanding of complexity is to use categories. This means that we look for similarities. Early in the history of chemical dependence treatment, researchers tried to group alcoholics and even their wives by suggesting that among them were common personality types. More recently therapists working in the chemical dependence field have tried to classify family members according to the roles they play in the family. Let's differentiate some often confused and confusing terms: role, personality, and self.

The concept of *role* has to do with social group membership. A family role applies to the patterns of behaviors that family members encourage and maintain for individuals within the family. We may also carry different social roles in groups outside the family. For instance, a recovering alcoholic parent may belong to Alcoholics Anonymous, his carpenter's union, a civic organization, and a church. Each group expects and encourages him to assume a functional role for that group. But these roles may contrast. If the president of a union, who openly discloses his problems at AA meetings, carried out the role behavior of an AA member in his union, his fellow workers might view him as dysfunctional.

On the other hand, *personality*, that is, our unified system of emotional and behavioral responses, *does* remain stable across groups. In fact, if an individual's personality were to change markedly from group to group, we would suspect abnormality. (Remember the famous story of Sybil whose *multiple* personalities led her into serious mental health problems?)

The *self* is the innermost core of our being. This is the part of us that each of us intuitively knows as "ME." We can experience our own inner state, but we can only infer the inner self of another. Sometimes, as in chemical dependence and co-dependence, we can become alienated from our own inner life. While the self implies continuity (I am always "ME"), it is also subject to flux and change. This is never more true than in the addictive disorders and with children from chemically dependent families.

Our external experience has a direct bearing on the inner self-experience. The various roles we play can either enhance or diminish our self. Concepts such as self-esteem, self-image, self-worth, self-confidence, self-reliance, and so on are all directly related to this inner "ME" experience.

When we enter recovery from chemical dependence, many of us experience the instability of the inner self, which can seem to change moment to moment, depending on our physiological condition. We rant and rave one minute; we become calm and settled after a good meal. When we're overtired or under stress, our inner experience fluctuates. If we don't live a balanced life, we find that we can become totally out of touch with our inner life. We feel an inner emptiness. We are numb.

Because of the wide fluctuations in the self experience, many of us begin to wonder whether or not we, like Sybil, have sixteen or so personalities. But personality implies *stability*. The lack of cohesion in our self-experience is usually explainable by the consequences of natural laws. We didn't get enough rest. We're hungry. We feel isolated and shut off from others. Or, something has just happened that has caused us to feel a deep personal insult. (In plain words, we're angry, and behind the anger is *hurt*.)

The importance of separating out the differences in role, personality, and self becomes especially important when we try to help our children. We need to know that behind any family role that a child plays, a child has a *real* self. And, although the child's personality is usually formed by the kindergarten years, our healing work must consider the inner self-experience.

Role Relationships in Chemically Dependent Families

Research in the field of chemical dependence has taught me about children of alcoholics and their family role relationships.[4] I began my first research in this area in 1974, and I've continued to work with recovering families and their children ever since. I've seen a number of these families over long periods of time. There is only one universal principle that I have found to apply:

> With the progression of the disease of chemical dependence, the formal role relationships in any family become distorted.

This means that the parents may exchange roles or one parent may assume all the responsibilities of parenting. One or both adults in the family may exchange roles with the children (role reversal), so that the children take care of each other as well as their parents.

As a result of the disease of chemical dependence, our perception becomes distorted. Through the haze, a parent may see one or more of the children as his or her exact duplicate (over-identification). Aspects of the parent's own self-image may be attributed to the child (role-projection). One child may be seen in terms of the parent's good qualities, while another child is seen as displaying the parent's more unfavorable qualities (split-projection).

Our unhealed wounds from the past also cause us to distort roles. We may project negative qualities from these ghosts of the past (a former spouse, siblings, or parents) onto our children. Role distortions operate more or less unconsciously, but they have a profound effect on disturbed family functioning. We can trace some of our problems with our children to these unconscious disturbances in family role relationships.

In recovery we need to realize that as parents we have had a lot to do with the family roles that our children play. However, we do not need to apply labels to these roles, such as the "family pest," the "perfect kid," or any other contrived label.

I don't want you to think of your child like so many other children. I want to assist you to free your child from whatever family roles may have become disabling. Consider the expression: "Labeling is disabling." This is never more true than with our children. Our public school systems are always under pressure to do away with the bias of labels that hold children captive. Research also informs us that labeling leads to close-minded expectations in school from teachers, peers, and even from the child who is labeled and at home from parents and brothers and sisters and from the child, himself or herself.

Now, I offer you my simplified approach to child development. *Our expectations will distort our awareness,* and we'll see what we believe and then believe what we see. This can be stated even more simply:

"What-you-see-is-who-I'll-be."

When we see something very special and worthwhile in a child, we foster the type of relationship that brings forth that child's personal best. If we close the lens of our mind and concentrate weaknesses, we may forever bind him to his limitatio

A family role can be a binding set of expectations for a child. Behind the role that binds is the hurt of the lonely, unnoticed self. This self of the child's innermost experience cries out silently, "What about "ME"?"

I want to help you recognize this message from your child's inner self, the self that still remains to be seen with all its special potential.

Sometimes you might have difficulty telling your children that you notice their specialness. You fear that your children will become spoiled or self-centered. But self-centeredness actually comes from *not* having been noticed and appreciated at certain key times during childhood.

If you were not recognized by your parents for the valuable, unique person that you are, you will continue to be the center of someone's universe. If you had to be a supporting player for your parent's alcoholism, you naturally will want to occupy center stage and be noticed for yourself. This was a *legitimate* need when you were going through certain stages of development as a child, and you're still trying to get that need met today.

Perhaps you did receive attention from your parent, but your parent's inconsistencies diluted the quality of the attention. Or, you may have been used by a parent inappropriately. You may have had to play the role of confidante or therapist to that parent when you really needed her to listen to *your* fears and uncertainties. The lack of parental support may have led you into dysfunctional role behavior. As you became an expert at playing your role, you became alienated from your inner, true self.

Automatic role behavior in a family can be a robot-like existence for the child who does not feel special. Childhood is normally that period of our lives when we are most spontaneous, carefree, and whimsical. Life is lived in the here and now, moment to moment. When you see a child expressing his unique self-potential, that child's eyes sparkle brightly. He is filled with wonder and enthusiasm.

Many of our children who are bound up in a family role look back at us with eyes that seem dull and ancient. They are lethargic and disinterested. A child may seem empty, lacking in zest and spontaneity, or so compulsively driven by the need to feel special that he is filled with intensity, tightly wound and constricted.

This rigidity shows up in the child's creative productions or in his play. To please others, he will produce exactly what is expected. When the child grows into young adulthood, he will begin to experience the deprivation of his empty inner self. He will find difficulty gaining satisfaction out of life. He then may tell us, "Sometimes I feel just like *I'm playing a role.*"

That is why I want all of us to know that parenting in recovery means a new way of *seeing*. We need to learn to look beyond the role. We want to see the hurt that may be in the eyes of our children, and we want to begin to acknowledge that hurt.

That's why we don't rush in and begin to "push those change-buttons" until we've allowed our child to teach us about her inner world. We don't want to begin to pull the strings of a puppet-child and encourage yet another role. Rather, we want to help our child begin to unfurl and blossom according to her own intrinsic nature as the one rosebud unlike any other in the garden.

Sometimes we are tempted to look for easy answers, for solutions, for a formula, or for an equation. But not just any equation, we want one that *works*. Unfortunately, the application of rigid principles to any human being just doesn't work. Why not? Because of *individual differences*. As much as we are alike, we are each unique. None of us is ever *perfectly* endowed. So there can be no perfect formula.

Recovery is about learning to accept ourselves and our children as imperfect human beings of worth and value. Our imperfections make us unique.

Our imperfect parenting leads us to search for a better way to be in a relationship with our imperfect children. The parent who places *value* on this *search* has already arrived, as far as I'm concerned. That parent already has begun to implement the most basic laws of healing.

Recovery also is about open-mindedness. We must be willing to change. So we'll need to guard against the kind of rigidity in our thinking that leads us to look for quick and easy solutions to complex problems. In parent-child recovery, we want to continue to revise and refine, from day to day, from month to month, from year to year, what we believe is "the problem."

What is true for one family in recovery can't always be generalized to every family in recovery. Not too long ago I presented a workshop in the southwestern United States on healing solutions for chemically dependent families. One member of the audience confused me by saying that his family consisted of six hundred members. (He was a Native American who lived on a reservation.)

Within our own Parents in Recovery group, there were key differences between the respective group members and their family size, culture, and structure. Karra was an affluent, single parent. Fred and Mimi were a more traditional, two-parent family in middle-class suburbia. Chuck was a blue-collar worker separated from his wife and children. (He didn't even know which direction his family was going to take in recovery: reunification, divorce, or continued separation.) Sam and Sara had been living in the subculture of urban street life among alcoholics, other drug-users, and pushers. Their son, meanwhile, has lived in a rural setting with foster parents and siblings.

What did these parents in recovery have in common? They shared *hurt*. They were bound together as a group by their deep, unspoken hurt about the problems that chemical dependence had contributed to their parenting. They were ready to speak out about that hurt. Perhaps they were struggling with denial or were fearful of reviving their own buried childhood hurts, but they were willing to learn. They were willing to struggle together to maximize their learning about how to heal the hurt of their children.

Sam was right, of course. The basic notion behind healing the hurt of our children is *parental love*. While this love can't be taught, the commitment to love can be improved.

First, we may have to transcend our own childhood hurt. Then, no matter what, we must find a way back to our children to begin to heal their hurt with our love. No other healing balm will ever be so effective. Parents in recovery are the most effective healers of their children's hurt. I have become so convinced of this that I encourage a model called PACT (Parents as Co-Therapists). I have stressed this model to professional helpers in my book, *Children in Recovery*.[1] During the course of working with a child, I also work with the recovering parent to help develop his or her natural therapeutic potential. This work with parents is essential. Children want and need their parents as their primary helpers, especially during the childhood years.

Our children need not grow up to be another generation of adult children who have to learn to heal themselves. We can initiate the work of healing now through our simple *acts of love*. Parental love is the principle behind healing the hurt of our children.

4 | The Hurt Beyond the Role

"So, how do we begin to see our children's hurt?" Karra asked.

"Just remember that a family role has a lot to do with the eye of the beholder," I replied. "You need to learn to look beyond appearances."

"Oh, that's your theory from last session on how kids fulfill their parents' expectations, even the bad ones," Mimi said. "Think about it, Karra. 'What-you-see-is-who-I'll-be.'"

"What you're saying is if I see Billy as a bully, then he's going to act out the role. And if I see Angel as a little witch, then she acts out her part, right?"

"Something like that."

"Then, it's *my* fault! I knew sooner or later we could expect to take a little guilt trip in this group. Alcoholic parents always get blamed. Well, I'm not buying your theory. It's too simple!"

"Hey, Karra, it just means that our kids hurt deep inside where we can't even see," Chuck suggested.

"Now how are we supposed to see what we can't even see? Really! This is getting ridiculous."

I wanted to introduce a way for the group members to begin to *see* in a new and different way. I didn't know how much each was being held captive by that legacy of hurt from their family of origin. This legacy keeps us shortsighted, able to see only what is right in front of us. Our own deeply buried, childhood pain can blind us to the present-day hurt of our children. Our front line of defenses—the false front—distorts our vision. The group needed a practical way of learning anew. I chose the following exercise to help them learn about their own ability to project onto others a variety of superficial roles.

Our Legacy of Hurt: A Family Dramatization

"Begin to imagine how you might view your own family's story if you saw it being portrayed in movies or on the stage. Would your story be a drama? A comedy? A farce? A tragedy? Where would you begin your story? Whom would you include among your cast of characters? What role would *you* play—heroine, martyr, villain, or a combination of these? Or, would you play some other role that you can think of from movies or novels or even television?

"What role would you assign to your children? You may want to borrow some role from fables or children's classics or fairy tales. Try to come up with *only one role* that is most typical for each child in your family. In the theater this is known as type-casting. You are also playing amateur psychologist as you start to look for specific types or categories.

"Your validation—proof of your ability to see beyond appearances—will be through what is known as consensual *validation*, that is, how much the other group members agree with you. The group will listen without comment while you tell your family's story, and then they'll have a ten-minute discussion in the back of the room. If they don't agree with your type-casting, they'll work as a team to come up with new characterizations for your drama. Are there any questions?"

"No. The game's a snap, but frankly I don't see how it's going to help," Karra said.

As the group members began to imagine their family roles, jotting notes, only an occasional nervous laugh broke the silence until Karra raised her hand.

"OK if I go first?"

The group prepared to listen to Karra's type-casting. "I'm definitely the heroine in my family. I've held us together through divorce and recovery. And I'd say I'm a success. I've cast my husband as the jerk or villain. What more can I say?"

"You can tell us about your kids," Sara said.

"OK, my Angel reminds me of this little poem I once heard about the little girl with the little curl right in the middle of her forehead. *'When she was good, she was very, very good, and when she was bad she was horrid!'* Now, Sandy is definitely *The Princess and the Pea*. You fellows know what I'm talking about? It's a fairy tale about this ultra-sensitive princess who has to be treated so special. That's my little Sandy, all right. OK, group, now's your chance to applaud!"

"But you left someone out," Chuck reminded her.

"I know—I forgot Billy. But I just couldn't think of a role for him—except one silly nursery rhyme that keeps going round and round in my head. I can't understand why I see Billy that way, so forget it."

"No, let's hear it. Billy needs a part, too."

"Don't ask why, but it's this:

Little Boy Blue, come blow your horn.

The sheep are in the meadow and the cows are in the corn.

Where's the little boy who looks after the sheep?

He's under the haystack, fast asleep.

Will you wake him? No, not I!

For if I do, he'll be sure to cry.

"OK, everyone, stop your laughing. I feel ridiculous. It's so silly." Karra broke into a spontaneous little giggle that seemed to erupt from deep inside her. Abruptly, she stopped. "Get to work, group. Your time!"

When the group took several minutes longer than had been allotted to discuss Karra's characterizations, she began to pace in the front of the room. "Aren't you finished yet? There's nothing to this game. Really! Just go with the first thing that comes to mind."

Finally the members returned to the circle. "I'm sorry it took us so long," Mimi apologized. "But the way you see *yourself* is too shallow. You're much more complex. But we were afraid to tackle you—assign you a role. We're all—well, *intimidated* by you, Karra."

Karra laughed, "You sound like my employees."

"Hey, no joke!" Chuck said. "If it weren't for Mimi, we'd still be sitting back there. We drew a blank on you, Karra."

"But then I got this flash," Mimi confided. "I told the group, and they said, 'That's it! That's Karra! She's Alice and the Red Queen.'"

"Alice who?"

"Did you ever read *Alice in Wonderland* or her adventures *Through the Looking Glass*? It's a children's classic."

"I never had much time to read to my kids. Work, work, work, you know. Angel reads to them. She's the bookworm."

"Well, I tend to see a lot of the world through children's books because I'm an elementary school teacher, as well as a mother," Mimi said gently. "Not that Alice is *only* for children. Adults can learn from it, too."

"Well, I'm not going to run right home and read it tonight. I'm waiting for you to tell me. So, get on with the story, Mimi."

"*Alice in Wonderland* isn't real. It's just Alice's dream. That's how the story ends, she wakes up from her dream."

"Then it's a bedtime story," Karra said sarcastically.

"Well, no, I never thought it made a very good bedtime story. Not for my girls, at least. It's all about confusion. And about what's real and what's not real. Alice even becomes so confused that she doesn't know herself. *Through the Looking Glass* ends with her saying that maybe what she saw through the glass was more real than real life."

"Mimi, I haven't the foggiest idea of what you're talking about," Karra answered, yawning. "Sorry. I'm not bored. It's just that you're telling me this bedtime story, and the hour is getting late."

"Alice is just a little girl," Mimi explained.

"You see me as a *child*?" Karra asked, suddenly alert.

"Well—also as this Red Queen."

"Don't tell me. Let me guess. It's my red hair, right?"

"Well—I suppose," Mimi said vaguely. "But it's more because the Red Queen is this powerful woman, a figure of royalty. And she is teaching Alice about this huge game of chess that's being played all over the world."

"How bizarre!"

"The Queen wants to teach Alice this game of chess—maybe, we could say it's the *game of life*. But Alice has such a hard time keeping up with the Queen. I mean, to learn this game, they have to run hand in hand. The Queen keeps pushing Alice to go faster, faster, faster. Alice is exhausted, and finally she just can't go on anymore. When she stops to rest for a few minutes, Alice is shocked because they haven't moved from the place where they started. They didn't really go *anywhere at all*—even after all that running!"

Mimi paused, but Karra remained quiet. She slouched in her chair, her face blank.

"So Alice confronts the Red Queen. She says something like 'After all that running to *get somewhere*, we stayed in the same place!' The Queen is very condescending. She says something like 'Oh, you wanted to *get somewhere*? Well, in my country, which I guess you could say is Wonderland, *it takes all the running you can do just to stay in the same place. If you want to get somewhere, you'll have to run twice as fast as before!*'"

"And, that's *me*? Pushing myself to the limit and *never* getting anywhere?" Karra's voice cracked. She leaned forward, collapsing into herself, hiding the tears that were now erupting from the dormant volcano of childhood hurt.

This group of strangers had seen beyond her false front to the childhood self that had been hidden for years. They understood the purpose of her constant striving to be noticed and admired. Despite her facade, the group cared enough to confront her. They recognized the role that had become second nature to her, the role of the Red Queen. Thank God they didn't accept her superficial view of herself in the heroine role. This was her own grandiose vision of herself, a vision that stressed her need for importance but denied her pain.

Mimi reached to embrace Karra, but Karra pulled away. The exposure was too sudden, too intense, and too threatening. That buried part of Karra—the injured child—had been trying desperately for years to get away from herself, to get somewhere else, and to *be* someone else. The tyranny of the Red Queen had been too great a price to pay. Like Alice, Karra had run out of breath. Exhausted, she finally began recovery. But the longer she remained in recovery, the more she realized that the Red Queen was back again, driving her to stay miles ahead of herself, now demanding that she be a perfect parent.

"I need help—some water," Karra pleaded, still not looking up to face the group members.

Sam brought a glass of water, but Karra didn't take it. She didn't drink. She just let him hold the glass for her while she wet a tissue and sponged her eyes. When she finally looked up at the group, her eyes had softened. The heavy mascara was gone. Her expression was sweet, childlike.

"You know me better than I know myself. Like how I've been running. For years. Twice as fast as I could for my own good. With all that running, I lost a part of me back there somewhere. You helped me find her tonight. I just wanted to say, well, thank you."

The group remained silent.

"I guess I've been running from my kids, too. I didn't want to get to know them—scared, you know—and I sure as hell didn't want them to get to know me. Little Billy has suffered the worst. Like me, he's had to hide out—under a haystack—you know? I've always been robbing him of his chance to feel special, to toot his own horn, so to speak. I hope you don't believe that I really *knew* what I was doing. I was blind—the victim of my Red Queen—my overinflated ego."

Then Karra made another personal request of the group. She asked for additional time to share her story. The walls of her false front had begun to crumble. She liked the sense of freedom that came from opening up about her past.

Karra's Story

"There's a reason I tried so hard to be a perfect wife, perfect mother, and powerful career woman. Little Alice thought she could get somewhere else and be someone else. As far back as I can remember I wanted to run away from home. That's my earliest memory, standing at the gate, trying to run away, to run after my old man. I saw him driving off early one morning when I was three years old, and I knew he'd never come back. I never knew why for sure, but I always thought it was my mother. Her filth. Her laziness. Who could stand her? I sure couldn't.

"We lived on welfare, but she couldn't even manage the money that came from the State to feed me and my brothers. She'd fill up our little old house with all this junk food and junk furniture, bragging about how she was going to make it big in the antique business and get us off welfare. Years passed and that old junk furniture just spilled over into the garage and even out to the street. So while she always made it seem like we had a lot of stuff, it was nothing but junk!

"Mom never seemed to notice. She prided herself on every piece of rickety old furniture. Even after it became dilapidated, she'd still be yapping about how it was a priceless antique, and she just needed to find the right buyer. Talk about denial! But I could see that it was junk, and I felt ashamed, like I was part of it.

"A lot of men came in and out of our house delivering furniture or coming to look at her priceless pieces and make her an offer. The offer usually turned out to be for a night in the sack. Some of them stayed for a while, but before long they'd get like the furniture, old and dilapidated. Mom was hard on men. But another one always seemed to come along.

"I craved attention from the time my dad left, and so I was a sitting target for some of those old men. I'd try to dance and pretend to be a ballerina or a princess, and the old man would laugh and applaud. Mom would overhear and she'd come rushing in. 'Stupid kid! Clumsy as her dad. A chip off the old block. Big Red was the clumsiest man you ever saw. Never could carry a piece of furniture without putting a dent in it.' Pretty soon the old man would be teasing me and calling me names, too, like Clumsy or Skinny or Freckles. And, he'd get the idea I was fair game for tickling or touching when mom wasn't around. I'd spend a lot of time hiding out alone in the garage behind some old bureau, like I was a fairy princess in my castle and one day I'd grow up to be a queen and live in a mansion.

"When I started getting older, I once told Mom about her old men touching me. She said I was nasty and filled with evil thoughts. So she pulled me by the arm down the street to an old preacher she knew, and he convinced her that I was filled with the devil. He told her, 'Most red heads are born that way. You've got to beat it out of them and pray it out of them when they're little.' So Mom stood there watching while the preacher beat me with his belt until my legs were raw. Then I was ready for his prayer treatment. He told mom she didn't have to stay, that he'd take care of me. Hah! He took care of me, all right. I was never the same afterwards.

"When I was nine, my brothers got to me. The eleven-year-old held me down while my teenage brother raped me. Mom refused to listen when I told her that her favorite son had gone all the way. She told me that he was only my half-brother anyhow, and besides, if I didn't keep my mouth shut, she'd take me back to the preacher down the street.

"My brothers got to me a few more times after that, but I got so that I was like steel on the outside. When they'd start bothering me, I could make my mind go off into my dreams while they molested me. I'd see myself as rich and powerful, living in a big mansion. I plotted. I planned. I schemed." Karra had been talking through gritted teeth, and suddenly she threw her head back against the chair and closed her eyes.

"Karra, are you OK?" Mimi asked. "Would you like another glass of water?"

Slowly, Karra sat up and looked around the room, releasing her grip on the chair. Her face was pale. "Maybe a cup of coffee. How about it, Chuck?"

Obediently, Chuck got up from his chair, left the room, and after a few minutes, returned with a steaming cup. "I knew you'd want it black."

Karra slowly sipped the coffee before she started to speak again. "Well, what better place to find a man to help me find my mansion than a real estate company? That's where I landed my first job as a receptionist. And it wasn't long before that Red Queen came into my life, and I got really fast. I stole this guy away from his wife without blinking an eye of guilt. Of course, it was only coincidence that he owned the real estate company. I convinced him that I was too young and too smart to stay home, even though he wanted me to start having babies. Instead I went to school to get a real estate license, and I started selling houses like crazy. I mean, I had this passion that was soul-deep about living in a nice house. And I could convince *anyone* that they needed a newer, bigger, or better house. With every property I sold, my head swelled the way my mom's used to do when she'd buy a piece of junk furniture. At last I knew the feeling that kept her buying. The *high*. I got so good that I went for a broker's license and then pressured Bill to make me a partner.

"You know what he said to that? He'd make me a partner in the business if I gave him a kid. Angel got me the business!

"But one kid wasn't enough. He wanted a boy. By then I was feeling pressured from him, and I resented it. 'So what's in it for me?'

I asked. 'Well,' he teased, 'maybe that little mansion you're always talking about?'

"So I got pregnant and gave him his son, Billy. But guess what? No mansion! He kept making excuses.

"And maybe that's when I started using more alcohol than usual, just to take the edge off. It worked. I felt even more powerful than before. I was a six-figure woman way ahead of my time. But life was getting more complicated. Stressful. Oh, I had this perfectly decent housekeeper for the kids. But the booze was making me nasty. I was suspicious of Bill and the business, like he was trying to hide things from me. So I got even more competitive. I was determined to edge him out.

"Well, he beat me at my own game—in a way I didn't plan. He started carrying on with this little flirt of a receptionist in our office, and everyone knew. History repeats itself, they say. The receptionist stole him out from under me the way I'd stolen Bill from his first wife. What a jerk! He filed for divorce just as I was ready to deliver Sandy. He accused me of trying to slip that one in on him, to hold him in the marriage.

"I started feeling more and more like I did back when I was a kid and the house was filling up with junk. I wanted to hide out behind some old bureau. But booze was the only fortress I could find. I honestly didn't know I was pregnant at the time I was drinking so heavily. God! It scares me to death to look back at what could've happened to my precious little Sandy. She filled up my life after Bill left.

"You know most of the rest of my story. I got the biggest divorce settlement you can imagine, and right after that I got myself a mansion. Oh, it's really just a mini-mansion. A big, beautiful house in the country. And it's filled with authentic antiques. But it's lonely and empty, and it never has really filled me up the way I always dreamed it would. But it was my fortress after the divorce. I'd hide out at night, drinking my vodka and doing my lines of cocaine. I mean, what else was I supposed to do all shut up like that in a big empty mansion? I needed to feel queenly, you know?"

"Do your kids ever visit their dad?" Chuck asked.

"Oh, yes, I let him have his little visitation strictly monitored, of course, through a children's service bureau. One afternoon, every other week."

"Geez!" Sam grimaced. "I feel bad for you, Karra, but what can I say? Maybe your kids need a little more time with their dad."

"Yeah," Chuck agreed. "I know he did you dirty, but they're still his kids."

"*My* kids!" Karra's steel door of defenses clanged shut again. "He divorced me *and* my kids! No way do I ever intend to let him have any time with Sandy. He's practically disowned her."

"Well, what about Billy?" Chuck continued. "That little guy might just need his dad. Maybe he's hiding out under that haystack like you used to hide out as a kid. Bet he sure is lonely for his dad."

"Thanks, guys, for trying to help. But my mind's weary. I've had enough for one night." Karra turned to me, "I'm ready to listen. So have at it. Maybe you could begin by explaining the point of that little game we just played."

The Family Puzzle

The point of the exercise on role projections is this: *A family role has a lot to do with the eye of the beholder.* One person's heroine may be another person's villain. In every family there are different perspectives, different ways of viewing the same problem. With a family of four, we may get four different perspectives. No one view is right or wrong; each view is just different. Each is valuable because it contributes to a more complete understanding of the overall picture. When we ask that same family (or group) to work together to come up with a consensus, we may even get a fifth perspective from the composite point of view. This is like putting together the pieces of a puzzle to form a whole picture.

Karra's Piece of the Puzzle

When Karra set out to copy an idealized lifestyle, she didn't realize that she would be pulled in so many different directions by so many clashing role behaviors. She married a man who owned the real estate firm where she worked as a receptionist. But in order to rise above the humiliation of her childhood, she needed more. Success became the driving force in her life. The Red Queen of her demanding ego always insisted that she needed to go a little bit faster, usually twice as fast as she could.

To go as fast as the Queen demanded, Karra turned to alcohol. To drive Karra faster and faster, the Red Queen whipped her with the fear of failure and the fear of poverty.

When Karra's less-than-perfect husband jilted and humiliated her, her illusion of a perfect world began to collapse. Just like all the other males in her life, her husband betrayed her. She covered her threadbare self-esteem with a cloak of false pride, supported by alcohol and cocaine. To hide her shame, she donned the mask of arrogance. To demonstrate her power, she bought her husband out of their business. To conceal her deep hurt, she became aggressive and demanding.

In recovery, Karra was finally able to admit that her ruthless career goals made her almost forget about her children, except for little Sandy whom she clung to at night. Desperately, Karra turned to the divorce baby to fill in her emotional gaps and loneliness. She reasoned illogically that alcohol would not be a problem for the baby who was sound asleep beside her as she drank. When Karra eventually passed out, she was safely huddled next to her infant.

The distortion in family roles occurred so gradually that Karra scarcely noticed. If she did, she didn't care. Relying on Angel to look after Billy, Karra praised the girl for being so mature, so obedient. Angel was the little girl who Karra had always wanted to be—a model of perfection, a straight-A child who didn't want for anything.

Karra fought bitterly in court to keep the children all to herself as though they were parts of her own body, as integral as her arms and legs. And, of course, these different parts of her very own person—Angel, Billy, and Sandy—would feel and think exactly as she did. When Billy dared to question her bitterness towards his dad, she would say, "Your father left US, so WE divorced him." (How easily Karra had forgotten about her own childhood longings for a father who disappeared overnight.)

So, Karra rigidly controlled the children's visitation with their father. She convinced the court that Bill was a loose, immoral man who had run off with a younger woman "strung out on drugs." (This wasn't true, but Karra could be a formidable and convincing parent in the courtroom.) After a while she began to believe her own lies, and she became convinced that Bill's new wife might offer drugs to the children.

The more Karra became alienated from the truth, the more she required chemicals to seal off the deeper layers of a self that was in constant emotional pain. She felt half a woman, a fragmented human being, held together by alcohol, soothed by marijuana, and power-driven by cocaine.

The chemicals began to confuse her. Through her distorted chemically induced vision, Karra began to see her son as she had seen his father. She didn't like the little boy she saw. She pushed Billy away with cutting words and rejecting actions. The more she told him how much he was a "chip off the old block," the more the echoes from her childhood ghosts came back to haunt her. The more she began to sound like her own mother, the more she resented Billy for her self-loathing.

Karra's Role Projections

A parent who unwittingly assigns a role to a child compromises that child's selfhood. The child comes to behave in concert with the projected role. The more Karra saw Billy as his father, the more the little boy began to act just as he was perceived to be. Desperate for his mother's attention, Billy acted out any part she assigned. He could be the "little jerk," or the "bully," or whichever characterization she applied to him, just as long as she noticed him.

A child's role behaviors can come to serve as a suit of armor to hide his hurt from the world. He can toughen up when what he really needs is to pour out tears of anguish. He can giggle away the tensions of his fears. He can wear a stubborn face when he is trying to cover deep shame. But the more we concentrate on the child's outward role behaviors, the more we lose sight of that child's inner self. Selfhood is, after all, more than the sum of the different roles we play.

To begin to see the hurt behind Billy's role, we'll need to tune in ever so sensitively. We'll have to experience the world as Billy actually does. We'll need to shift our perspectives. Let's attempt this now as we concentrate on Billy's inner world.

Billy's Piece of the Puzzle

Lone warrior in a family that has been fractured by divorce and dependence, Billy has suffered early loss and rejection. He first lost his mother to her career, then to a new baby sister, and finally to her dependence on chemicals.

His father left when Billy was only four. That was the same year that he lost his mother to the new divorce baby. He hated the screaming infant. He was sure that the divorce baby had driven his father away. The raging, red-faced Sandy took his father's place in bed, right next to his mother. The divorce baby reminded Billy of a monster.

Sometimes Billy would awaken in the middle of the night, dreaming of monsters. He'd cry out for his mother. Angrily, she'd finally come into his room and flip on the light switch, holding a glass of vodka.

The ice clinked in the glass as she lectured him: "You're driving me to drink! You're jealous of Sandy, admit it!"

"No, mom, there was this monster over by the closet—"

"Monster? You're the monster, Billy. You *and* your dad. Both of you, driving me to drink."

The more vodka she drank—a second and then a third glass—the more menacing she became. She'd sit and rock in Billy's little blue chair and glare at him, continuing to lecture.

"Jealous of your baby sister, aren't you? Well, *you don't have a right to be*. Look at your room, full of toys." She'd get up and start to kick the toys around the room.

"A closet full of clothes!" She'd pull out a few of his shirts and trousers and throw them on the floor.

"And your own television set!" She'd turn on the television full blast. "What more do you want, *you little monster*?" she'd scream.

Scrunching under the blanket and covering his ears to shut out the sound of her mad voice and the blaring television, Billy would finally fall into a fitful sleep while she was still raging, just like the divorce baby.

Early the next morning as the sun rose, Billy would awaken with a tightness in his stomach. He would peek out from under the covers. Sometimes his mother was still in his room, passed out and slumped nude in his little blue rocker with the vodka glass broken on the floor.

He'd tiptoe around the broken glass, running into his older sister's room where he'd climb into her bed. Snuggling next to Angel, Billy felt safe, warm, and protected. Later, when the time came to get up, they'd creep into the kitchen. Before the housekeeper came, Angel would grab the whipping cream from the refrigerator and pour out bowls of crisp cereal, squirting the cereal with globs of whipped cream.

They'd giggle while she made a mountain of the whipped cream. Waiting hungrily, Billy would tell Angel about his mom's crazy vodka-talk.

"She's just like a witch when she's drunk," Angel would say out loud. They'd laugh together with their secret about their mom. The silliness made Billy's stomach feel better.

Growing braver, Billy would whisper almost out loud, "What if she *really* is a witch?"

Angel would laugh, thinking he'd made a joke. But Billy was serious. (He could never settle the question in his mind.) *What if his mother really was a witch?*

The minute his mother awakened, she'd stagger into the kitchen and start to cast a curious spell on Angel. Billy would watch Angel change right before his eyes. Her smile would disappear as her face became blank, almost like no face at all. Then, she'd scurry about to please their mother—brewing coffee and pouring out the bloody-red juice, splashing it with bitter hot sauce, a witch's brew. Who else but a witch would want a bloody drink? His mom called it a "Bloody Mary."

"Thanks, sweetheart," his mom would say to Angel cunningly, gulping down the drink. "I needed that little eye-opener." And then she'd turn to Billy scornfully. "You better get in there and clean up your room. It's a mess! Things thrown everywhere!" He was always too afraid to tell her that *she* had made the mess!

Billy didn't understand how Angel could fall under the spell of their mother's black magic. Behind her back, they could laugh, share secrets, and call her names. But just as soon as his mother appeared, she could control Angel without words. Angel would seem to be in a trance, under their mother's spell, with no mind of her own.

That's how Billy learned that he couldn't really trust Angel. Like everyone else in Billy's world, Angel could turn on him at any given time. He just didn't know when. He had to be on guard, just in case. He was convinced that no one could escape his mother's black magic. She had sent his father away. She had persuaded the judge to keep his father from coming around. Billy vowed that he would do everything he could to keep from falling under his mother's spell.

By the time he was nine, Billy had grown so tough that he didn't need Angel anymore. He argued with her frequently and called her names. He had stopped needing his mother long ago. When she went away to treatment, Billy didn't even miss her. He felt relief. A cheerful little song kept going through his head, "Ding-dong, the witch is dead;

ding-dong, the wicked witch is dead. . . ." As he teased and taunted five-year-old Sandy, telling her that their mother was never coming back again, he hummed the song to himself. He was too afraid to sing the words out loud for fear he might cause her to die.

At this time in his life (a time when most little boys his age look to their fathers in hero worship), Billy's model for adulation was some-one his mom still called a jerk. Even her treatment didn't cure her of that affliction. So Billy kept secret his wish to be just like his dad. Somehow, just as witches are prone to do, his mom guessed his secret. She exposed him once again. "You're a chip off the old block," she kept saying even after she'd stopped drinking vodka.

But one day Billy stopped feeling ashamed. In fact, he stopped feeling anything. He didn't care if she called him a jerk or a bully or a chip off the old block. He noticed that she seemed to like him when he acted that way. (Why else would she talk about it so much?) That's when Billy had guessed her secret, something he should have known all along: *If he became just like his father, then one day she could divorce him, too.* Billy puffed out his chest and played his role to the hilt.

The Misery-Go-Round-of-Hurt

Billy didn't choose his family role. He didn't suddenly wake up one day and say to himself, "Wow! I'm from a chemically dependent family that's gone berserk. My sisters are the good guys, so I'll just take the black-hat role for myself to grab some of the attention."

Billy's role in the family was the result of complex relationships between the different members of the family, but he was especially vulnerable to his mother's role projections. Billy could never make up for the hurt that his mother experienced during her own childhood, nor should she have expected him to perform this function for her. According to Karra's type-casting, Billy was like all the other males in her life—a betrayer. This legacy of hurt blinded Karra to Billy's real self needs and bound him to a role. The little boy was only dimly aware of his misery as he acted out the bully role.

Billy needed his mother's acknowledgment that he was an individual of worth and value. But how could she give what she had never received? Her own unmet childhood needs blinded her to Billy's need for love and acceptance.

And this is the law of the Misery-Go-Round-of-Hurt:

> We tend to do unto our children
> that which was once done to us.

The tendency to repeat the past is what I refer to as the Misery-Go-Round-of-Hurt. The law binds us only when our childhood hurt has been sealed away by denial. The law of the Misery-Go-Round-of-Hurt is based on unconscious conflicts still percolating below the surface, threatening to erupt at times when we least expect an eruption.

We can heal our own hurt while we learn to see through to the hurt of our children. A supportive group of recovering peers, such as a Parents in Recovery group, will assist us to bring clarity to our vision.

You see, there is one generic hurt, which Karra and Billy shared. This is the hurt that binds parents in recovery to their children and makes them capable of deep compassion.

This hurt can actually serve as an empathic resource as we enter into a healing relationship with our children.

And this is the hurt of all hurts:

> To be parented by people
> who sometimes treat you as though
> they really don't love you at all.

5 | Learning to See Your Child

"How can I heal the hurt of my children when I'm not even allowed to see them?" Chuck asked abruptly.

A week had passed. Tonight Karra sat apart from the group, noticeably subdued.

"Hey, Karra, sorry for blurting out like that. You OK?"

"I want to keep quiet and listen, keep a low profile. So, go right ahead, my friend, take the hot seat!"

Chuck cleared his throat, his voice trembling. "I've been wondering—why do I keep coming to these meetings? What's the use? My wife still won't let me *see* the kids."

"Take her to court," Fred offered boldly. "Get visitation spelled out legally."

"Hey, I can't make waves. If I so much as push Bitsy, she'll jump at the chance to file for a divorce, then fight me tooth and nail for the kids."

"Aren't some of your kids almost grown? Old enough to make their own decisions about seeing you?" Mimi asked.

"Things are a lot different today," Fred persisted. "An alcoholic parent can get reasonable visitation. So, take her to court."

"Before I'll vote for that, I'd like to know what Chuck *did* to make his wife so angry," Karra broke her vow of silence, moving into the group circle.

"*You'd* be thinking I had another woman. Well, I didn't!"

"Oh, but you did! *Booze* was your mistress," Sam insisted.

"What do you expect?" Karra asked. "You sober up like Mr. Nice Guy, but she's mad as a hornet over all those lost years. I'll translate *her* message of hurt. 'Hey, Buddy, who needs you *now*?'"

"Weren't you gonna keep quiet tonight?"

"You're starting to grow on me, Chuck. I want to help. I mean, after all the help you've been giving me lately!"

"Karra, you're too much!" Chuck shook his head, smiling.

"Just call me the Red Queen."

"I really *am* a nice guy—when I'm sober. My wife just won't take a chance on getting to know me sober. For that matter, I'm not sure I know her anymore."

"More lost souls," Sam said.

"Yeah, I guess. We started out as friends in junior high. By high school, we were getting serious—married a few years after graduation. I was just back from Vietnam. She'd just finished her nursing school. Well—eighteen years and five kids later—a lot of water went under the bridge."

"So who's this person you call 'My Wife'?" Karra asked.

Chuck stroked his mustache, looking perplexed. "She's a nurse. Takes care of long-term cancer patients."

"That's her *role*. Her job. Who is *she*?"

"She's one angry lady, that's who she is," Chuck sighed. "Now, back in high school, she was one *cute little thing*. Sweet, but shy. And I was a big varsity jock who made her feel protected. She'd say, 'Chuck, you're *perfect for me*!' She looked up to me, ya' know? After we started dating, she really blossomed. Tried out for cheerleader. Made that. Said she'd never felt so special. Said I made her feel *great*. Naturally we started spending all our time together."

"Naturally," Karra said.

"Over the years, my wife changed."

"Doesn't your wife have a *name*?" Karra asked.

"Betsy. Or, Bitsy. She's tiny, ya' know? Bitsy is my little pet name for her."

"She doesn't sound like your little pet."

"She used to be. Guess the longer we were married, the stronger she got. Me, I seemed to get weaker."

"Booze," Sam said. "Booze weakens you—steals your manpower."

"The first year of marriage was one big honeymoon. We partied all the time. Then, talk about bad luck. All at the same time, she finds out she's pregnant and my plant has a layoff. To top that off, her dad dies of alcoholic cirrhosis. That's when she started freakin' out. Said she couldn't trust me to take care of us. Called me a wimp. Said we'd have to move over by her mom and sisters so they could help out. I went along with it, her being pregnant and all.

"Us being on welfare really got to her. I knew I'd eventually get rehired. But she got on working graveyards at the hospital and kept right on going 'til the baby was born. Then, bang! She handed the kid over to her mom and kept on working. 'Gotta buy this, gotta buy that for the baby,' she'd say.

"A couple of years later we had twins. A boy and a girl. Cute kids. I was back on at the plant with a steady job. But she farmed the twins out to her sisters who lived across the street, and she kept right on working. 'Not enough of this, not enough of that,' she'd say. I got to thinking she didn't want to be around *me*. Soon as she'd come home in the morning, I'd be out the door for work. I'd get back, and she'd be into her sleep time before her shift started. Our house was empty. Life was empty. I just couldn't take it. So I got into the habit of going down to the corner bar every evening for a few beers, a few laughs, ya' know?"

"Didn't you get close to your kids?" Fred asked.

"I tried. God knows I tried to get close to my boys. But her sisters and mom got them into art and music. Weird stuff, ya' know? So I wound up getting real close to our eleven-year-old girl. Too close, my wife used to say. But I was so damn sorry for that kid. Betsy resented this child from the get-go. Blamed me for the pregnancy. Said she didn't want any more kids. Talk about *crazy*! A few years later, she wanted to *adopt* this baby boy."

"Is that the boy who took *your* place in bed?" Karra asked.

"I just couldn't keep Betsy satisfied. She was so—restless. I'd go along with anything. Anything to help our marriage."

"Don't tell me. Let me guess. Nothing helped," Karra said.

"My drinking got bad. So bad they laid me off as shop foreman. Betsy lit into me and told me to beat feet until I got the drinking 'under control'; I went straight to AA, and I'm sober now ten months. But she still won't have me back."

"Hey, man, she said to get it *'under control!'* Period," Sam said.

"Which I did. Period."

"Naw. Sober is *too* rad for her taste. Like, she might have to, well, *relate* to you. Get it? She married a young jock, party animal. And, you—well, you're middle-aged—a sober dude that makes her feel blah!"

"Don't you believe it! You're a well-preserved hunk," Karra teased.

"Let's not lose the point, here," Mimi interrupted. "I mean, we really should help Chuck understand more about being co-dependent."

Mimi's tentative style made her comment seem a perfect non sequitur. The group members stared at her with annoyance. But her perception of the issue was keen. Co-dependence *was* relevant to

Chuck's marital problems.

Chuck waved his arms, signaling frustration. "C'mon. No more new terms. You'll get me even more confused. My AA buddies tell me to *'keep it simple.'*"

"The Program also tells us to keep an open mind. Get rid of old ideas. Be willing to listen and learn and change," Fred reminded him.

"OK. OK. So, who or what is this *co-dependent?*"

"*I'm* a co-dependent," Mimi answered proudly. "Not on liquor, that's for sure. But I've got my share of dependencies."

"Yeah? Like what?"

"Oh, like being dependent on people. My kids. Fred. Even to Fred's alcoholism. I could always *use* his drinking to make myself feel necessary. I'd try to control his intake by hiding his bottles, watering down his gin, rationing his beer—"

"Hey, this is sounding like home!" Chuck grinned.

"Co-dependence is a kind of 'fix-it syndrome,'" Fred explained.

"The only trouble was," Mimi continued, "I was fixing everyone except myself. I couldn't see that the whole thing was getting out of hand for me—that *my* life was getting unmanageable."

"What kept you from seeing?" Chuck asked.

"A lot of dependencies! My job—where I had all these little fourth graders who were so dependent on me. I liked feeling needed. That equaled importance. So I'd work long hours, all without pay, to convince myself that I was important. Then I'd come home exhausted and blame Fred *and* his alcoholism for my unhappiness."

"It worked. I drank out of guilt sometimes," Fred admitted.

"Well, his drinking did make me unhappy. But I was overly dependent on my home, too, like he was his alcohol. That's why I worked, I mean, to fix up this lovely, show-place home that would be a reflection of ME—so people could rave about ME—about me being a fantastic homemaker and all. I'd entertain at home, but then Fred would come along and mess everything up with his sloppy drunkenness." Mimi glared at Fred, but he merely shrugged. "So I'd just occupy myself with all the entertaining to cover up for him. I fooled myself into believing that I was a real social butterfly. But, you know something? I was actually scared of people. Why—before treatment—you'd never catch me spouting off like this to a group of strangers, not that you're really strangers anymore."

"My wife's a nurse, and she's worked around people for years."

"You can work around people without ever feeling at ease with them," Karra explained. "I should know!"

Mimi continued, "So, I learned I was dependent on all these *things.*"

"What kind of things?"

"Oh, all the pretty odds and ends for the house. Or clothes. I could spend a whole day shopping. I'd drag my daughters along whether they wanted to go or not."

"*Our* daughters," Fred interrupted.

"What? Oh, yes. Well, back then I didn't know they were *ours. My* girls were a reflection of *me.* Just as though they were part of me. So I didn't feel right about myself unless they had all these pretty things, too. I used to think I was so concerned with their needs, but then I went to treatment and learned that behind all this co-dependence it was just *me, me, me.*"

"My wife's never been a shopaholic," Chuck said. "Couldn't afford to be—with five kids plus my drinking."

Mimi laughed good-naturedly. "A real dyed-in-the-wool co-dependent can get overly attached to the basics of life. Like to food. I guess you can see that I still *use* food. Too much. Too often. I'm trying, though. After Fred got sober, my girls started to rebel. They said they'd *never* felt close to me, just controlled. I cried for a week. But then I could see their resentment. That pain was worse than the pain of letting go. So, now I want to set them free—to see them each as separate."

Sara was tapping her foot impatiently. "I can't relate to this co-dependence jive. Or setting your kids free. Me and Sam have the one boy, Seth. No way can we set him free. That's why he got picked up by the cops and taken to foster care in the first place. He was too free."

I tried to help Sara understand that co-dependence is an issue for chemical dependents, too. *Remove the alcohol or other drugs, and a need still exists for healing the Co-dependent Self.*

"Give me a break! Me and Sam are addicts through and through. We can even relate to some alcoholics. But to co-dependence? No way!"

"So, a pecking order!" Mimi laughed. "You chemical dependents are a cut above us poor co-dependents, is that it?"

"I'm not like *you*, if that's what you mean. I don't get all stoked over little pretties for the house. Or clothes. Me and Sam kicked all our dependencies. We've gone totally vegetarian in recovery. No more nicotine or caffeine. We're mega-clean! I won't cop to co-dependence."

"What's all this WE-stuff?" Fred asked. "Could be you're dependent on Sam, only you don't admit it. Think back to street life. Weren't you both co-dependent with all your drug buddies and drug connections? You needed each other just to survive, like one big glob of co-dependence."

"Not the same. Not the same at all," Sara insisted.

"Denial!" Karra said. "Sara is *so* co-dependent she's in denial."

"Hey, Red Queen, who asked you?" Sara said before turning to me with eyes that were pleading for a rescue.

"Maybe my wife is dependent on her cigarettes. Not that those are the basics of life. But she smokes like a fiend," Chuck admitted.

"Hey, man, that's *chemical* dependence," Sam corrected. He leaned forward in a mock imitation of sharing confidential information, speaking in a half-whisper, "Haven't you heard, man? Nicotine is a *drug*. So's caffeine. Like you can get off on those drugs right in your own kitchen, and who's gonna narc on you? The stuff's *legal*."

"And maybe my wife's co-dependent with the kids. Maybe she wants them all for herself. OK, I guess I've known that for years. I felt shut out of the family, so I drank. But why would she want to shut me out now that I'm sober?"

"Let's see—" Mimi began vaguely. "I thought there was a connection."

"A tight connection," Fred said. "Like a Mama Octopus with her tentacles wrapped around each of her babies and them all entwined with her and each other. And, you can't tell where one stops and the other starts."

"That's the way *Bitsy's* got herself and our kids all wrapped up with her mom and sisters. And me, I got pushed out of the family, like I was one too many. I didn't fit in after the adopted boy came."

"It all seems so long ago, but, yes, it was like that with me and our children, too," Mimi confided. "I thought I was protecting them from some unknown disaster. From Fred. From his alcoholism. When he got sober, I got panicky. I wanted to run, too. Then, I got stubborn. I told myself that he wasn't going to move in on my territory just because he'd stopped drinking. Getting unstuck from my daughters was painful, too, and I didn't think I could stand it."

"Did you?" Chuck asked.

Co-dependence Revisited

Sara's defensiveness kept her from asking the one question that might have helped her help herself: "What is co-dependence?" Although this relatively new term is fast becoming a household word, folks who begin their recovery outside a formal treatment program may still be confused. So, what *is* co-dependence?

My answer is simply a common-sense observation: Co-dependence has been present among us forever, since the beginning of time. But only recently have we labeled the condition. We've discovered nothing new; only expanded our awareness.

Think back to the story of creation where the Garden of Eden is a lesson in antiquity. Eve was dependent on Adam for her very life. Then she became her husband's chief enabler, wanting him to gain more power from the forbidden fruit that would make them like gods. In the moment that Eve felt the need for that external, power-giving substance, the grandiosity of co-dependence was born. But, as is true even today, partaking of the external source of power did not bring potency. Instead, Eve lost power. Self-absorption and shamefulness followed.

From this original model of family dysfunction, we learn how self-centeredness (or narcissism) leads to family suffering and disruption. The original adult children, Cain and Abel, carried their bitter sibling rivalry to its extreme with violence and murder.

Despite this original portrait of family dysfunction presented in the story of creation, mental health efforts over the years failed to emphasize the need for family treatments. Only the most disturbed family member received therapy. Chemical dependence treatment followed this pattern until about forty years ago when we began to extend some help to the couple. Unfortunately, some of the first descriptions of the "CO" of this "COuple" were sexist and pejorative for wives of alcoholics.[3] But over time, we came to view the spouse of the alcoholic from different angles and perspectives, some of which were more objective measures of personality traits or role behaviors. Each viewpoint has helped us put together a mosaic of the syndrome that we now call "co-dependence."

The earliest descriptions of this syndrome were limited to the partners of alcoholics or addicts. A growing camp of chemical dependence specialists came to see "something" in their treatment settings that they referred to as "co-dependence." But the mosaic has lacked mortar because no unifying theory holds together the different pieces of the various perspectives. There also was sufficient disagreement between the views so as to pose problems in reliability. This means that if several observers were to look at the mosaic, they might agree that, yes, this was co-dependence; however, each would emphasize a different aspect of the mosaic. A reliable set of criteria will enable us to arrive at a common decision or conglomerate view in order to see the whole picture in a unified sort of way.

Today we are much closer to being able to classify a co-dependence disorder, which can be communicated to others. Outside the field of chemical dependence, other mental health professionals are embracing this concept as an important one.

The Disorder of Co-dependence

Today we have arrived at the place where we can talk about co-dependence as a specific disorder that requires treatment and recovery. In my opinion, the first person to propose a credible disorder was Dr. Timmen Cermak.[4] A firm theoretical basis supports Dr. Cermak's assumptions. He offers reliable diagnostic criteria. Any one of us could scan these criteria for ourselves and arrive at the same conclusion most of the time about whether or not a given individual is suffering from co-dependence.

Another important contribution from Dr. Cermak is to afford respectability to co-dependence among mental health professionals. Those outside the chemical dependence field can use the criteria to spot the disorder in their clients. They can communicate with a common language, which is neither vague nor filled with the jargon of the chemical dependency field. In fact, Dr. Cermak proposes that his criteria for co-dependence be included in the diagnostic manual that is the "bible" of mental health professionals.[5]

As I distributed a handout of Dr. Cermak's criteria to the members of the Parents in Recovery group, I emphasized that Dr. Cermak's view of co-dependence is especially important because it equalizes the distinction between chemical dependents and co-dependents. Thus, the "pecking order" that Mimi observed is eliminated. Chemical dependents, such as Sara and Chuck, can look at the list of criteria and make their own decision about whether or not they are co-dependent. They don't have to defend against the more threatening confrontations of their recovering peers. The criteria speak to us in a fairly objective way.

Criteria for Making a Determination of Co-dependence*

A. *Self-Esteem Problems:*

"Continued investment of self-esteem in the ability to control both oneself and others in the face of serious adverse consequences."

B. *Self-Alienation:*

"Assumption of responsibility for *meeting other's needs* to the exclusion of acknowledging one's own."

C. *Self-Other Boundary Issues:*

"Anxiety and boundary distortions around *intimacy* and *separation*."

D. *Self-Destructive Relationships:*

"Enmeshment in relationships with personality disordered, chemically dependent, other co-dependent, and/or impulse disordered individuals."

E. *Three or More of the Following:*

"1. Excessive reliance on *denial*

2. Constriction of emotions (with or without dramatic outbursts)

3. Depression

4. Hypervigilance

5. Compulsions

6. Anxiety

7. Substance abuse

8. Has been (or is) the victim of recurrent physical or sexual abuse

9. Stress-related medical illnesses

10. Has remained in a primary relationship with an active substance abuser for at least two years without seeking outside help."

(Italics mine.)

---

* Adapted from Cermak, Timmen L., M.D. (1986) *Diagnosing and Treating Co-dependence*, Minneapolis: Johnson Institute Books, 11.

The Co-dependent Self

I shared with the group my notion of co-dependence as a *disorder of the self*. An emphasis on the *self* draws our attention to two simultaneous events: *our self in relation to the external world of other people, places, or objects* (which can be observed) and *our inner experience of that relationship* (which *we* may or may not be able to recognize and which is usually unknown and unseen by others).

An example: Mimi works overtime because she thinks she is important and needed "by all those little fourth graders." Her *inner experience,* however, is one of exhaustion and irritability. She translates these events in the following way: "*I am important and needed* by all these little fourth graders. But I am working so hard and I am exhausted and irritable because of Fred's alcoholism." What Mimi discovered in recovery is that her translation is false. She has learned that she pushed herself in order to buy "all the little pretties" for the house so that she would be admired as a "fantastic homemaker." Mimi's life was mechanical. She became her roles. In the process, she alienated herself from her inner experience.

My simplified definition of co-dependence is that it is a *disorder of self-alienation.* We become divorced from the important world of our inner experience, or we retranslate the messages of this inner world to mean something entirely different. The retranslation usually suits the needs of our false front, the various roles we play.

Co-dependence is also a *disorder of self-cohesion.* The false front has been built up from our need to please others, and so it ruptures easily. With any slight hint of criticism, disappointment, or failure from others, we experience a sense of fragmentation as though we are falling apart. What happens then? *We blame the other person. We reject the other person.* Chuck's wife, Betsy, is a case in point. Pregnancy is a time when a woman feels most vulnerable. Chuck's layoff from his job and her father's death intensified Betsy's feelings. She attributed her severe feelings of insecurity to Chuck. He had failed her. She could no longer trust him to take care of her. Rejecting Chuck, she demanded that they move back to her old neighborhood to be near her mother and sisters.

Co-dependence is also a *disorder of self-esteem regulation.* Our self-esteem involves self-worth, self-confidence, self-image, self-satisfaction, and other aspects of our inner self-experience. Co-dependents look to other people, places, or things for their value and worth. Low self-esteem can fluctuate widely between grandiosity (feelings of importance, power, control, etc.) to rock-bottom-low where we experience ourselves as helpless, unworthy, and unimportant and feel ashamed of who we are. We have difficulty stabilizing around a midpoint between these two extremes. A more cohesive self-esteem would lead us to see ourselves realistically most of the time. We would know that we always have value, but that we also have human limitations.

Another important aspect of co-dependence has to do with our inner world. *We experience other people, places, or things as a psychological part of who we are.* This means that we look to important others to make us feel whole, complete, special, important, and powerful. A spouse, children, lovers, friends, and other members of the extended family help us feel cohesive. Alone, we feel apprehensive, restless, dissatisfied, unhappy, and empty.

When we experience another person as a psychological part of ourselves, we assume that we know what the other needs, wants, or thinks; we expect the other person to know precisely what we need, want, or think. We experience great disappointment when the other person disappoints us by not knowing what we need, want, or think. This poses grave problems for our relationships in general, but especially for our children.

Most folks aren't mind readers. So unless we communicate our expectations clearly and directly, others will invariably fail us. (Even when we do communicate directly, they won't always carry out our wishes perfectly.) When we experience another as a psychological part of our selves, we look to that important other to provide meaning to our lives. Away from that person, we feel incomplete and empty. Chuck talked about his experience of this emptiness when he arrived home to an empty house at the end of the day. When his family let him down, he sought consolation in other places and things: the corner bar, alcohol, and his beer-drinking buddies.

Any of us in Chuck's position might have experienced inner distress. But if these important, inner messages are to be of value to us, we must linger with them rather than flee from them. If Chuck had lingered with his emptiness, he might have interpreted it this way: "Something is drastically wrong with my marriage and family life. I've got to find outside help so that we can correct the problem."

But Chuck followed the path of self-alienation. He ran from his inner messages to seek immediate relief at the corner bar. We can always run away from ourselves, of course, and that is what co-dependence is all about. Our flight can be to the shopping center, to food, or to a pill. But our flight simply transforms and intensifies the urgency of our inner messages, which now become compulsive symptoms.

I'd like to reemphasize the importance of two levels of experience—*the inner* and *the outer realm of self-functioning.* Co-dependence is a type of twisted conduit that results in twisted communications between these two worlds.

As parents in recovery, we need to recognize that our children also will operate at these two different levels of self-experience. In order to begin to see our children clearly, we need to see beyond our own self-alienation and co-dependence to theirs.

Co-dependent Parenting

For almost two decades now, I have worked with children from chemically dependent and other dysfunctional families as well as with adult children in recovery. I continue to learn about the severe and subtle ways that we parents hurt our children, often without realizing what we are doing. I have found that when a parent brings hurt to a child it is because that parent often suffered similar hurt in childhood. We may not even remember the harm that was done to us when we were children.

But we know in general the different types of harm that result from chemically dependent and abusive families: *physical abuse, sexual abuse, family violence, neglect, abandonment, and psychological abuse.* Regardless of the type of abuse, there is one core hurt common to each. This is the hurt that also results from co-dependent parenting.

The selfhood of the child is neither
recognized nor affirmed.
The child is not even seen as having a self
that is separate from the parent.
Rather, the child is experienced
as a psychological part of one or both parents,
as his unique self is denied.
The child is valued only for the functions
that he provides or for the roles
that he fulfills for the parent.[1]

Co-dependent parenting fosters the same type of self-alienation in our children that has been present in us.

Today we have the opportunity to begin to heal the hurt that may be present in our children. But in order to see our children clearly, we need to move a step beyond our own co-dependence. We need to seek support from a community of recovering peers who will be familiar with our struggles because they, too, have lived them. Being open with each other as parents in recovery will challenge us to new levels of caring about our children.

Chuck's opening question to the Parents in Recovery group bears repeating: *"How can I heal the hurt of my children when I'm not even allowed to see them?"* Certain of us share Chuck's dilemma. But, as Chuck came to realize, even if he had remained with his family during his early months of recovery, he might not have been able to really "see" his children. His co-dependence limited his ability to see them distinctly. Any parent who is separated from his children can use the time apart to move beyond co-dependence. This paves the way for the parent to begin to see the child as a separate self. Then, parent-child reunification affords the opportunity for the parent to begin to respect and affirm the child's unique self-potential.

6 | Who Will Heal Their Hurt?

We can help.
But as much as we love a child,
We can never give to that child,
What a mother or father can give.
— Mother Teresa of Calcutta
1979 Nobel Peace Prize

"How can recovering parents be expected to heal their own kids?" Karra's emphatic question opened the final group discussion.

Next week the series on "Healing the Hurt" would begin. Each of the group members wondered if they would be able to implement the principles of healing. How could they help their own children whom they had harmed? As usual, Karra's concerns were the most intense.

"I've been listening week after week to chemical dependents and co-dependents. We're all in the same boat—just trying to keep afloat in this big sea called Recovery. I say our children need help from *real* professionals, *not us.*"

"What's wrong with *us*?" Sara asked.

"What's wrong? We're still in need of help ourselves, that's what's wrong! How can we start healing our children?"

"Like maybe a counselor should heal their hurt?" Sara continued.

"Yeah," Fred joined in. "Or a priest—someone who knows how to help. I'm just starting to learn to be a *parent*, not a healer."

"Not *every* professional knows how to help," Mimi said. "Back when Fred was still drinking, I went to a psychologist and he—"

"You what?" Fred interrupted, stunned.

"Oh, don't get excited, Fred. I didn't go to snitch on you! Or, maybe I did. Anyhow, I thought I was going for our son's bedwetting problem. I did mention your alcohol problem—how it was causing stress for the whole family. But that doctor talked right over me, ignoring the alcohol problem, telling me that all I needed for our son was this blanket device with a buzzer to wake the boy up in the middle of the night so he could go to the bathroom. I was to keep this daily chart to record his wet and dry nights. The psychologist called it 'Behavior Management.' Well, just thinking about one more responsibility on top of what I already was doing made my head start buzzing."

"I sure don't remember a buzzing blanket or any management chart that you kept."

"No. I didn't buy that darn buzzer thing. And, as for keeping that management chart—why, it was all I could do to manage my own life back then. I didn't go back to that doctor either. I still feel resentful when I think of him. I guess I needed him to listen to me about the alcoholism—"

"You *guess* you needed him to listen," Karra said. "Talk about co-dependence! Mimi, you are the Queen of Co-dependence."

"Hey, there must be counselors out there somewhere who know how to work with our kids," Chuck said, turning to me.

"Counselors don't wave a magic wand, ya' know!" Sam said.

"Besides, we're talking something else here. Like healing the hurts that *we* caused our kids."

"Karra's got us so tweaked-out we don't even know what we're doing," Sara said. "First she was into changing her own kids all by herself. Now she's saying we're all too messed up to even help our kids. Personally, me and Sam think our recovery has got to include our kid. We plan to help him the best way we can."

"Why, Sara, dear, you are light years ahead of the rest of us in recovery. Do invite us to your graduation when you get your family all healed," Karra said.

"Cool it, ladies!" Chuck said with annoyance. "I'd lay bets that we all have cold feet about healing our kids. If my five kids walked in here right now, I wouldn't know what to say."

"It only takes two little words: *'I'm sorry,'*" Sara insisted. "Then, when you really get wound up, you can stretch those two out to a dozen. *'Hey, kid, I'm sorry I hurt you with my drinking and using.'*"

"That won't work with my kids!" Chuck said. "No 'Sorry' is gonna heal a seventeen-year-old young man who used to get belted in my alcoholic rages. I had so much resentment for that kid—my oldest—just because he didn't like sports. He spoiled *my* fun. He couldn't throw a football. Dumb stuff like that. I'd hear him plunking on the piano, and I'd guzzle down a can of beer while I ran around the house looking for chores that weren't done—just so's I could belt him. Yeah, I know that sounds sick. But I hurt my kids real bad." Chuck wiped his face against his sleeve as tears filled his eyes. Still talking through his own hurt, Chuck seemed to shrink in size as he relieved some of his immense burden of guilt.

"I rejected my twins, too. Oh, sure, I love them all. Deep, deep inside, I love my kids. But the twins just didn't seem like *my* kids after awhile. Seems they rejected *me*. They always got baby-sat by their aunt across the street. She's an artist with her studio at home. Makes a pretty good living at it—pottery, weaving, and big abstract oil canvases. So my kids got exposed to all that stuff, and my boy-twin really picked up on it. I guess he's got some talent. But anytime I'd get a little too much to drink, I'd abuse him. *Mentally.* He'd bring me some fantastic little drawing, and I'd just smirk.

"'What the hell is this?' I'd say. 'And who the hell are *you*? Guess you belong to that lady across the street. No son of mine wastes his time drawing pictures all day.'

"Alcohol had my mind so warped at the end of my drinking that I thought Bitsy's family was the enemy, plotting to turn my kids against me. I saw my kids going over to the other side, just like her family had stolen them from me.

"Sometimes I'd ridicule my boy-twin so bad he'd run out the front door, back to his aunt's across the street, and I might not see him again for a week. Then I'd yell at Bitsy about how they were all in on the plot. Hell, I can see now that her family didn't steal my kids; they were protecting them. I drove them away with my cruelty.

"For some reason, my girl-twin could talk back to me. She's sixteen going on forty, I guess. A little know-it-all. 'Sassy' is my pet name for her. She can cut me to shreds with words. She'd say, 'Keep your big mouth shut when you're wasted.' Once she even accused me of being weird with her little sister, Cindy. That's my eleven-year-old, the one I'm closest to or used to be. Once, just before I got thrown out of the house, Sassy told me, 'You oughta keep away from Cindy when you're wasted. You get weird, huggin' up against her like she's your girlfriend. You're just plain weird.'

"Imagine hearing your teenage girl lecture you with hate in her eyes. Accuse you of things like that. I'd just laugh, hide my shame, and accuse Sassy of being jealous. 'Jealous? You *are* weird! I'm not jealous. I'm *ashamed*. Ashamed you're my dad.' Sometimes Sassy could sound just like her mom, just like Bitsy, and I'd get all confused when I was drinking about who was really who in my own family.

"So, there you have it, Sara. I don't think 'Sorry' could ever set it straight with that bunch of kids over at my house."

Sara waited, making sure that Chuck was finished before she

offered support. "Hang in there, big guy. You've got more honesty after ten months sobriety than most people will ever have. One day you're going to be able to help your kids."

"Hold it, there's more. And this part is the worst. It's about me and that adopted boy. I've resented that kid ever since he came into my life, and I don't *want* to make it up to him," Chuck's jaw tightened, and his voice was suddenly hostile. "I resent that adopted boy so much right now—right while I'm talking to you, that I could walk over there and punch holes through the wall. Damned if that little brat didn't steal my place in bed! No way will he ever get so much as a 'Sorry' from me. Sure, I'm ashamed about my real kids getting hurt by me, and I want to help them. But, I'm just too filled with hate to heal anybody."

"We're all in the same boat," Fred tried to console Chuck. "We feel inadequate."

"That's it. We're all *inadequate*," Karra said smugly. "That's what I meant before. We're just *too inadequate* to heal our kids."

"Hey, Karra, you really tick me off when your Red Queen gets all puffed up like that," Sara said sharply.

"Oh? You like me better when I'm sniveling? Now, tell me, dear Sara, my Queen of the Streets, what's *your* Big Plan for healing that poor little Seth from his early exposure to dopers and pushers and pimps and prostitutes back when you and Sam were strung out every day? Just how do you plan to heal your son from all that?"

"No *Big Plan*," Sara answered calmly, nondefensively. "We're just loving Seth with all we've got inside our two big sober hearts. Like, you may not know it, but me and Sam are devoting our sober lives to really loving and helping that one little boy. That's the plan."

Karra, for once, was speechless.

Parents as Healers of Their Children

The Parents in Recovery group was on the threshold of beginning to work with the hurt of their own children. Each member had joined the group for that specific reason. They had traveled together through weeks of sessions on denial, messages of hurt, roles, and co-dependence, and they had learned. They had moved through their own denial to an awareness of the need for healing. They had opened their eyes gradually to an understanding of the importance of healing the hurt of their children.

Now, like actors who have been preparing for the opening of a play, the members were expressing reluctance—a type of stage fright. They didn't feel equal to the profound challenge of encountering— perhaps for the first time ever—their children with truth.

The group members needed reassurance. Karra's argument that a "perfect" time exists for parents in recovery to help their children had swayed them. According to Karra, the time to help their children would be when each parent was perfectly healed, free of all inadequacies. If we followed Karra's line of reasoning, most of us would wait for some ideal moment in the future—and that could take a lifetime.

Karra's Red Queen seems to dictate a type of healing that we might label "Either/Or." *Either* we are perfectly capable and whole, in which case we can help our children; *or*, we are completely inadequate, and we shouldn't even bother. But recall that Karra's Red Queen lives in Wonderland, where perspectives can be rather topsy-turvy. In the real world, we need to be wary of extremes. *The ideal time to begin healing the hurt of our children is NOW.*

But, Why Parents?

Certain group members, such as Karra, Chuck, and Fred, were still blinded by their inadequacies. They were stuck in self-centered fear. They did not realize their potential to be loving, healing parents. An intellectual argument would not convince them of their importance as their children's healers. So, I proposed a puzzle. This was actually the same enigma that I had encountered some twenty years earlier when I began to wonder about children of alcoholics and how they coped with life. When their parents were involved with chemicals, these children often had to cope alone without parental support and guidance. But what happened after the parents began recovery? Did that parent suddenly become available to the child as a source of comfort and guidance? Or did the child continue to cope alone? What did the child have to say about his or her need for help?

I wasn't interested in external or behavioral measures of a child's so-called "dependency strivings." I wanted the child to direct me to a better understanding of his or her *legitimate*, but unmet, needs for support and guidance.[6]

My original puzzle was this, and now I posed it to the parents in this recovery group. I asked them two questions:

1. Whom do children of parents in recovery *actually* experience as their helpers during times of stress?

2. Whom do these same children *prefer* as helpers in times of stress?

Originally, I believed—as I still do—that the answer to these two questions has a lot to do with the way we construct helping relationships for our children in recovery.

Potential Helpers for Children During Stressful Life Events

Self	Favorite Teacher
Mother	Physician
Father	Clergy
Brothers	Counselors
Sisters	Favorite Pet
Good School Friend/Peer	Favorite Toy
Relatives/neighbors	No One
Other Adult Helpers	

In my original study I offered the above names to the children as prospective helpers during a variety of stressful life events. The stressful occasions were those that children often encounter—sibling difficulties; school problems; physical injuries and illnesses; feelings of embarrassment, fear, shame, anger; and so on. First, I asked each child in an individual interview to identify her or his own unique life stresses and to name who actually helped during each event. Next, I asked each child to review these events again and tell me the name of the helper(s) whom they would have *preferred*.

Originally, the results of this study surprised me. Now I asked the Parents in Recovery group to form their own hunches or predictions about whom the children really preferred as helpers. Karra still was convinced that most children would want to receive assistance from a professional counselor. Mimi said that, in her experience as a teacher, children frequently sought out the classroom teacher in times of trouble. Chuck believed that relatives might be preferred over parents. Fred was convinced that children would actually prefer the help of a loving spiritual leader, such as a member of the clergy. Sam and Sara stated that most children *preferred their parents* as helpers, regardless of the parents' previous failings.

Children of Recovering Chemically Dependent Parents and Their Experience of Helpers During Times of Stress[1]

Actual Helper	Preferred Helper
NO ONE	PARENTS

Above are the findings of my original study. When I shared this information with the Parents in Recovery group, they were puzzled. What did it mean, they wanted to know, that the *actual helper* had been "NO ONE"?

My original prediction was that the children would most often name the "Self" as being the actual helper. I expected each child to report that he or she had coped alone in precocious acts of self-reliance. But what the children told me about their inner experience was that, while they may have coped with stressful life events alone or even with the assistance of some other helper, they continued to feel an inner lack. Something—someone—vital was missing.

The NO ONE Syndrome

What the children helped me understand about their inner dilemma was that even capable, competent children can look good to an outside observer. They accept responsibility; they cope; they survive. But deep inside, when life is threatening or overwhelming, the child experiences the profound emptiness of the NO ONE Syndrome.

The other part of the syndrome has to do with the childhood need for support and affirmation from parents. A child will not be able to express this need for the parent with words. He or she will experience an inner longing. Emptiness. A void. The child will not always recognize that the source of this longing is for his very own imperfect parents to comfort and reassure. During the teen years, this unmet need is transformed through the maturing defenses of defiance and pseudo-independence. By the time of young adulthood, denial of this need for parental love is complete. The memory now shifts to the abuses and injustices of childhood that were committed by the parent.

The adult child's experience of "NO ONE" will still be there as an inner void. Emptiness. But now there is a frenetic search for something outside the Self to fill the black hole. Too often a chemical starts to be used because it works. The NO ONE Syndrome is anesthetized. The hole is filled. And, if in later years, you ask an adult child how he or she coped during childhood, you may hear the answer, "Oh, I took care of everything and everyone all by myself. I was *responsible*, you know." That same adult child will not recall his childhood experience of the NO ONE Syndrome. The memory has shifted. The imperfect parents have been rejected. (Who ever needed *them* in the first place?) Denial sets in. A desperate search begins to find perfect people, wonderful places, or just the right thing to fill the void. You rarely hear an adult child tell you of his longing for his very own parents. He has become too adept at fooling himself. (Denial works.) Rarely will you hear about the void, the black hole that was never filled with the right quantity or quality of parental love.

But when we turn to little children, they may not be adept with words; but they are very much in touch with their need for love and comfort from their parents. Regardless of our failings, our children still look to us to help them heal their hurt—even from the very abuses which *we* have inflicted. Our children may look like they are coping and actually helping themselves or each other. But in reality they feel that no one is helping them, no one is present for them. And whom do they long for, whose help do they seek? Ours.

The Natural Healing Potential of Parents in Recovery

Today I work with recovering parents to help them develop their natural therapeutic potential. When I recently asked a little eight-year-old client what her parents could give her that no other helper could, she yelled out the answer—LOVE! Even though little Maria lives in a foster home, abandoned by her drug-addicted mother, she knows that her mother still *loves* her in a way that no one else can.

Parents are unique as healers of their children's hurt because they can offer *love*, a mysterious love that is inherent in the parent-child relationship. I don't pretend to understand this love, but I know that I've experienced the mystery of a deep, abiding love for the special human being that is my child. The communication between a parent and a child can be so deep and profound that it transcends time and distance.

Over and over again as I've worked with children and their recovering parents, I see that love heals. If our children continue to long for that spirit of love that only a mother or a father can give, then we parents can contribute something very special to our child's healing.

We can mobilize the hurt from our own painful childhood experiences. We don't want to overidentify and confuse our hurt with that of our children, and vice versa. But we can use our own hurt to become deeply empathic. *Empathy* has to do with self-forgetting; we momentarily relinquish our own point of view and we look at another's experience through his or her eyes.

Finally, we can use the freshness of our experience as recovering parents: We are helpless and vulnerable when we start out in recovery. When we feel overwhelmed by stress, we want to lean upon a supportive friend. When we seek a sponsor, counselor, or other friend in recovery, we learn that healing comes from their empathic attunement to our distress. The deeply receptive person who assuages our own NO ONE Syndrome nurtures us.

Healing the hurt of our children is about putting our love into ACTION. Now. If we shy away from helping our children because we're not perfectly healed or recovered, we'll miss some of the most important opportunities for expressing our love.

As we grow with our children in recovery, we can demonstrate our commitment in the face of our own limitations and struggles. We'll be teaching our children that we don't shy away from problems or deny them when the going gets tough. This is a most important lesson for children in today's world. Our children need to know that to live life is to have problems. Recovery offers us new problem-solving abilities, and we can actually make an art out of sharing these with our family through the process of day-to-day living.

We teach our children that, despite our failings, we want to improve. We want to become better human beings.

We can let go of that storybook existence of our childhood dreams and realize that it was our child's-eye view of an alternative to our family dysfunction. Today we want to stop lamenting about our family of origin and all its failings. Recovery teaches us to go forward. Today, we seize the opportunity for learning the lessons that were never taught to us as children. We become creative and avid learners, and we use our knowledge to heal the hurt of our children.

Creating a Functional Family

A few years ago I conducted a workshop on the topic "Creating a Functional Family." Before beginning the workshop, I asked my audience how many of them had actually grown up in a "functional family." Many of the audience were professionals, some in the field of chemical dependence. But only a couple of people in that entire group of about five hundred raised their hands. All the rest confirmed by the nodding of heads and a later show of hands that their family of origin had been "dysfunctional" in some way.

So as parents in recovery, we must not feel alone or somehow jaundiced by our past experiences. We don't go from being dysfunctional to being functional overnight, particularly when our learning is based on dysfunctional rules. But if we have no functional rules to bring into our own families, how can we learn to be effective parents? Do we read books and magazines or attend some type of school to learn to be more adaptive?

If we are parents in recovery, we have a wonderful forum for learning functional rules. We can learn these rules by the same system that is applied in our *twelve-step families*. We begin to apply functional principles to our relationships with others.

Even though most twelve-steppers have grown up dysfunctionally, they can pursue learning these twelve steps as a new way of life. "Working" the steps means applying the principles behind these steps in our day-to-day living situations. The steps are based on some of the most profound principles of healing to be found in various spiritual and philosophical traditions. These steps do not correspond to any one "religion," but they do contribute to physical, mental, social, and spiritual growth.

Today I would say that the twelve-step family is the single largest "extended family" in our history. An individual from the East Coast, for example, is immediately at home in a twelve-step meeting on the West Coast or in Hawaii or in Europe and most other parts of the world.

A few years back I saw a conference advertising a certain psychological therapy in lieu of twelve-step programs. "Who would design such an alternative?" I questioned. Usually the option is proposed by someone who hasn't walked a mile in the moccasins of the recovering chemical dependent. We *need* to belong to a healing community of recovering peers to help overcome the isolation and the alienation of chemical dependence and co-dependence.

More recently, I heard a learned man (who is also outside the chemical dependence field) comment about the power that can be found in the twelve-step programs. "When the story of this century is written," he said, "it will include the importance of the twelve-step programs to healing our world." Do we need to look for options or alternatives? You decide.

In my book *Children in Recovery*,[1] I discuss the application of the twelve steps to parents in recovery. In Chapter 12 of *this* book, I offer another translation specific to helping you heal the hurt of your children. I hope that supportive Parents in Recovery groups will begin to make use of these steps as they offer self-help to each other.

7 | Legacy of Hurt

"Do you still think you need to run away from your family to stay sober?" Sara was speaking to Fred, trying to keep the group alive as they waited for Chuck's arrival.

The members shifted nervously, impatiently. Earlier that evening, everyone had been enthusiastic, ready to begin the first class on "Healing the Hurt." Now with the delay, tensions were building to the point of threatening group disruption. Sara wanted to preserve the group's cohesion. So, she brought up Fred's leftover topic from the first meeting. The theme was relevant to the group's immediate experience. And Karra picked up on it.

"Speaking of *running away*, I think Chuck has run out on us. Just like a man, they'll bail out on you every time. Oh well, Chuck's lost his kids, so he doesn't need us anymore. I vote we get started. Chuck, wherever you are, may you rest in peace." Karra crossed herself in mock reverence.

"Now, don't be so quick to judge," Mimi cautioned. "We can't abandon Chuck. We've become his substitute family. He needs us. He wouldn't drop out without letting us know. I vote that we at least give him a call." Mimi turned to me, "Do you have his phone number?"

While I was looking through my desk drawer for Chuck's file, Fred continued with Sara. "What made you ask that question, about *me* wanting to run?"

"You brought it up—weeks ago—but you haven't mentioned a word about it since. Has our group helped you get over those feelings, or what?"

"Most of the time I want to stay with Mimi and the kids. Other times these waves come over me, and I start to feel like I'm closed in, I can't breathe, and I want to run. It's like I'm being pushed and pulled, pulled and pushed, and I don't know why."

"Fred has a problem with closeness," Mimi sighed.

"Don't we all," Karra agreed.

"It can be tense in a family. Real tense when you're starting to open your eyes to everyone's needs. I used to have three cute little girls in lace and ruffles—and Mimi, of course—but one day I wake up in sobriety, and I've got a little boy and three gorgeous teenage gals who always need something. Well, it can be—tense."

"Fred's more at ease with our son," Mimi said.

Just at that moment, the door opened and Chuck came bounding in, breathless from running up the stairs.

"Hey, sorry I'm late!" Chuck was smiling broadly as he took his chair, unaware of the group's tense mood. "Gosh, so much has happened, I hardly know where to start."

"Look, man, this isn't a discussion meeting," Sam said with annoyance. "Like we were supposed to start our first class tonight."

"Hey, that's right! Some memory I've got after all those years of drinking. But so much has happened lately, I just gotta bring you up to date. A few more minutes—that's all I'm asking."

The members realized that something important had changed for Chuck since the last meeting, and Sara, Mimi, and Fred were immediately in favor of letting Chuck have the additional time. They finally convinced Sam and Karra to allow Chuck to tell his story.

"It all began a couple of nights ago. You might say, all hell broke loose. I'm sound asleep when the phone wakes me up, ringing off the hook. It's Bitsy. She's hysterical, calling me from work, crying and begging, 'Please, hon, please get over to the house quick.' I didn't know if I was asleep or dreaming, but then I heard her say, 'Something terrible has happened to our kids.' I came awake real fast. She said she'd just got this call from that little adopted boy—our youngest son—who was at his Grandma's house next door to ours, trying to get help. He musta been scared out of his wits. Bitsy's mom wouldn't do a thing to help. She musta froze up with fear herself, being elderly. But Bitsy was mad as a hornet at her ma. 'That's just like her,' she was ranting and raving, 'Ma never could stand up to Papa when he was drinking. She's let me down again. Please, hon, I need your help.'

"Seems the kids' baby-sitting aunts are over in Europe now, so Bitsy's been trusting our teenagers to care for the two youngest kids this summer. No reason she shouldn't. The oldest boy is eighteen now, legally an adult, and the twins are sixteen. But come to find out, them older kids have been heavy into alcohol and other drugs all summer, partying at night at our house when Bitsy goes off to work. The little ones have been too scared to snitch. But that night things got bad. Real bad. So the adopted boy had to do something.

"Bitsy keeps begging me for help. 'Please, hon, even if you've got hard feelings towards me, I don't blame you. But just remember they're your kids too. They need your help. They need a man to stand up to them.'

"Me, I got over there as quick as I could. I walk into our house— the first time in almost a year—and the place is a shambles.

"It's dark. Morbid dark, except for the porchlight and some candles they've got going inside. I could make out all these kids dressed in black with weird-colored hair, like nothing I ever thought I'd see in my own home. Heavy metal music was blaring. I don't know why the neighbors didn't call the cops, except, come to think of it, mosta them neighbors are Bitsy's relatives. And you already know her ma wouldn't do anything.

"Tell you the truth, I felt like running myself. I saw my oldest boy, he's got some girl pinned up against the wall, he's almost pounding her face to a pulp, and them other crazy kids are cheering him on! Godalmighty! I got dizzy and had to back out of there. I ran out to my car, ready to drive off, thinking to myself, 'You don't need this.' Then I heard Bitsy's voice in my mind. 'Chuck, be a man. Don't be a wimp. Stand up to the kids.' So I told myself, 'If you let her down now, Bitsy's never gonna forgive you.'

"Some fierce rush of courage came over me, I ran back in there, and I started turning on lights and blowing out candles. My oldest looked around and saw me, and he started coming for me half-crazed, like a bull that's just seen red.

"Something flipped in my mind, like a VCR switch on reverse, winding back to when he was a little boy. And when he started to swing at me, I saw *me* swinging at his little boy's face and him begging me, 'Don't. *Please, Daddy, don't. Don't hit me again.*'

"'Sorry, Buddy,' I told him this time, 'but you and me gotta have one last round, and I can't let you win. You're dangerous, son.' So I grabbed his arms and threw him to the floor, and then I fell over him and kept his arms pinned down just like he'd pinned that girl to the wall. He was kicking and cussing and calling me names.

"'Call me anything you want,' I said, 'cause I probably deserve it. But don't take it out on some poor, innocent girl.' I looked over and saw that girl laying limp on the floor. Fainted. Passed out—or dead. I prayed to God that she wasn't dead, but her face was one bloody, awful mess. I just started yelling for Cindy, my youngest girl, not even knowing if she was home. But sure enough, she'd been hiding out in a closet upstairs, scared to death.

"When Cindy heard my voice, she came rushing down the stairs looking at me like I was Superman. I told her to get on the phone quick and get me some cops and paramedics over here.

"Now you won't believe what happened next. I'm still holding down my kicking and screaming boy, and I look up to see my twins grinning down at me, puffing on weed, like they were watching a comedy. I screamed loud enough to bring them to their senses. I said, 'You two better get this house cleared of drunk kids and dope, or I'll have the whole bunch of you thrown in jail.' I meant it too, twins included."

"Are your twins in *jail*?" Mimi asked with disbelief.

"Naw. They beat feet over to their grandma's after they got them kids outa there. By the time the cops came, the paramedics had already been and gone. They took that poor girl to a hospital and my son straight to a treatment center. I reported to the cops about my son abusing that girl. Maybe she'll press charges. I hope she does.

"First thing next morning, me and Bitsy went over to the treatment center to sign our son in for as long as it takes. Booze and speed, that's his problem. A pretty bad one, from what they told us at the center.

"Then we went right home, loaded up the twins, and drove straight back to that treatment center. We got them enrolled in an outpatient program. They're not as bad as their older brother, but we told them, 'You complete this program, or you'll be on the lockup ward with Buddy.' They were scared. Even Sassy kept her mouth shut for once.

"You wanna talk about guilt and hurt? I've had to face up to being responsible for three kids on alcohol and drugs. I've fathered three young people right into chemical dependence."

"Don't be so hard on yourself," Mimi said. "If chemical dependence is a family disease, then it's passed on from your wife's side of the family, too. And you had to get it from *someone*."

"Darned if I know. I started out life in an orphanage. Never knew a thing about my real folks. They may have been drunks. I was in this one foster home where the dad was a bad drinker. He abused me a lot, and I got filled with hurt and bitterness. I never felt like I was worth much until my last foster family in junior high. They got me into sports. I started feeling like I was good to somebody then. Being the star athlete, I was important to the team and to the whole school in a way. They needed me. Then, along comes little Bitsy, and she made me feel like a giant. Still does.

"Somewhere I've got me a twin brother. But he got adopted when we were babies in that orphanage. Me, I got left behind. Something wrong with me, I guess. Why else would one of a pair be left behind? I've always had this terrible grudge against my twin brother for cheating me out of a better life. He stole *my* place. He got himself adopted."

"Chuck! Did you hear yourself?" Karra asked with a sudden flash of insight.

"Hear myself *what*?"

"You just explained why you've had so much resentment against your adopted son! Think about it."

"My mind's just gone blank. You'll have to explain."

Seeing that Chuck's mood had suddenly changed and that he was confused, Karra urged him to forget her interruption and to continue with the story about his children.

"Well, I'm real proud of that little adopted son of mine. He's earned himself a hero's medal, far as I'm concerned. He's definitely on my good side now. It was one hell of a night, but in another way, it was a miracle night. The change in Bitsy is a miracle. She's telling me that she shouldn't have kicked me out. She should've stood by me while I went to get help for my alcohol problem. She said she knows our boys needed their dad around—they needed me there. She's mad because she was so blind to their drug scene this summer. Why, she's even blaming herself for working the night shift all these years and letting me down as a wife. Never thought I'd live to hear her say that.

"But the best miracle is that Bitsy and me are back together. Even with all this trouble with our kids, we've been a couple of lovebirds the last few days. She said I'm back like I used to be, like the guy she married."

"Recovery does bring miracles!" Mimi said.

"Oh, there's still more, and this will blow your mind. Remember, Karra, you once said Bitsy needed this group? Well, I told her."

"Terrific. And she told me to butt out of her life, right?"

"Heck, no. She listened. She wants to come to our group. Can she crash our meetings?"

"Certainly," Mimi said. "Tell her to join us next week."

"Next week? Hey, didn't I explain that Bitsy's here right now, waiting outside the door? She wants to get started tonight. Is it OK?" Chuck turned to me, suddenly remembering that I had something to do with structuring the classes that were to begin on "Healing the Hurt."

I announced to the group that I thought we should delay our series until the following week. Meanwhile, I introduced some important family principles that also influence relationships with our children. These seemed especially relevant to Chuck and his wife as they began family reorganization in recovery.

When Chuck walked back into the room with a small, pale woman on his arm, he introduced her as his "Little Bitsy." She seemed to cling to the big, sturdy fellow, as if she wasn't strong enough to hold herself up or to be the mother of teenage children. She seemed childlike in the roundness of her face and her petite, underdeveloped body. But a different message came from her deep-set, gray eyes. They showed an ancient weariness, the kind that comes from having lived centuries or from working many years of sleepless nights on the graveyard shift.

Perfunctorily, Bitsy took her place in the group, nodding to each member as she was accustomed to doing in nursing staff meetings where supervisory role behavior dictates decorum. Even now she couldn't step out of that rigid role. Her voice was impersonal, mechanical. "I feel that I know you. My husband has told me about this group. I'm deeply impressed that you are so dedicated to making a better way of life for your children."

Bitsy continued in a monotone, congratulating the group as though she was awarding a service recognition to her staff of nurses. A long silence fell heavily over the group. The members didn't know what to do with her formality.

Bitsy looked down at the floor. "I asked to come to this group for myself because Chuck told me that someone—I don't know who—was kind enough to invite me. I *do* need your help. I've got to learn to reach out to my children. I've done so little for them over the years, except try to give materially. Chuck tells me that our older children's problems mean that they're filled with hurt. I'd never looked at it that way. I was thinking that they were turning out bad. Just like their father—I mean, the way Chuck was before recovery. And just like their grandpa, my father.

"Papa died of alcoholism right after we were married. I'd always thought I hated him; but when he died, I was brokenhearted. I've feared his alcoholism for myself; and then, when Chuck's drinking got out of hand, I couldn't deal with it. History repeating itself, you know? So I fled into my work. Thanks to all of you, Chuck's turned his life around—the way my papa never could do."

When Bitsy looked up, her eyes were moist. She was showing a glimpse of the deep hurt that had been behind the weary eyes.

Karra reached out to shake Bitsy's hand. "I'm Karra, the one who invited you. Now sometimes you'll hear this group call me the Red Queen, but that's just their little pet name for me. But I don't think we have to use your husband's little pet name for *you* here.

"To us, you're *Betsy*, your own person. And I want to welcome you person to person, parent to parent, a sister in recovery. We're all here to help each other help our children."

Behind the Scenes:
The Family Processes of Recovery

Processes are those unseen influences that govern our relationships with a group of people. Processes have less to do with the exact words that are spoken or the actions that are taken than with the patterns of these interactions. In every group, certain patterns keep the group alive or cause it to fall apart. Let's examine the processes at the opening of the group meeting at the beginning of this chapter.

When Chuck's unexpected absence began to create a negative climate in the group, Sara sensed that the group was splintering. She spoke words to Fred that contained a message to the entire group: "Let's continue to work together as a team."

Karra's impulsive response to exclude Chuck may have been her way of covering over the anxiety she was feeling—the revived abandonment fear. Typically Karra kept these feelings buried by rushing headlong, like the Red Queen, *to get somewhere else.*

If Karra had succeeded in excluding Chuck, she might have fragmented the group. And that's exactly what happened in Chuck's own family. His exclusion led to family breakdown. *Processes are those interactions that keep the group alive and cohesive or cause it to break up and fall apart.*

The processes in our own family are continuously changing, pushing and pulling us towards some pattern of growth and change. Usually we're so caught up in these processes that we don't see them at work. We're so busy contributing our part to the workings of the whole that we can't sort things out clearly. Like Fred, we feel as though we're caught up in some invisible revolving windmill of powerful, unseen forces.

The Recovery Windmill

We can use imagery to symbolize the processes of our changing family in recovery. Try to visualize a windmill with three blades of different sizes and three equidistant spaces between the blades. The different-sized blades correspond to the relative amount of time that our families will spend in a particular recovery phase.

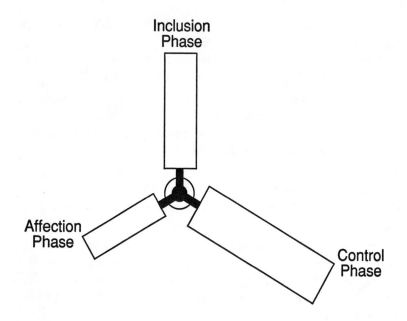

The first phase of recovery is the middle-sized blade. This blade represents the period of recovery or what I call the *Inclusion Phase*. The second phase is the largest of the blades, representing the middle or *Control Phase*. The smallest blade symbolizes the period of intimate family relating known as the *Affection Phase*, which occurs during long-term recovery.[7]

The Recovery Windmill helps us grasp the significance of the workings of the family processes of early, middle, and ongoing recovery. As we pass through each of the phases of recovery, we'll slip in and out of the spaces between the blades. I visualize these spaces as those periods of "Family Relapse" that are expectable and predictable.

The Inclusion Phase

The central question of the first period of recovery is one of *belonging*. Who is in and who is out of this family? The recovering parent often experiences ostracism. "Do I even belong to this family anymore?"

Recovery does bring a major shifting of family membership. The chemical dependent in our family may enter a treatment center, become involved in a twelve-step program or outpatient program; or utilize some other recovery resource. As this occurs, each family member is asking the unspoken questions: "Where do I fit in? What does it mean to belong to this family in recovery?"

The Family Relapse Cycle

When the family consolidates membership, a period of calm and stability occurs when everyone experiences belonging. Then, almost abruptly, the whole family begins to act as they did in early recovery. People withdraw from each other or become suspicious and guarded in their interactions. This period of resistance or backward movement is predictable. Our family has fallen into the spaces between the wind-mill blades, trapped momentarily in a kind of wind tunnel of chaos and confusion. Just as we can't see the wind moving the windmill, so we aren't aware of these forces acting upon us. However, we do *experience* them, and we do feel the results.

The Family Relapse Cycle is made up of the tensions and fears that keep us stuck in a certain phase of recovery. We resist growth and change. But *what* particular aspect of growth and change are we resisting?

Once the family has been established as a solid group, the members will have to decide *who is in charge* of this family in recovery. Thus, control issues and power struggles now emerge, and the family resists these conflicts.

The Control Phase

In the field of chemical dependence, *control* has become a negative word. Yet psychologist W.C. Schutz emphasizes that all human beings have the need for a sense of control or mastery over their lives. In the chemically dependent family, the normal control motives usually are distorted. We need to remember that fear motivates control. Out of desperation, children may have assumed family leadership. Or one parent may rule with aggressive dominance, while another uses subtle, manipulative control.

Leadership doesn't have much to do with the natural role positions of being husband or wife, mother or father. *Leadership* is a *function*. Whoever is carrying out that function at any point in time is acting as the leader of the family. When a child has been forced into a family leadership role in order to survive, the parent's abstinence is *not enough* to convince the child to relinquish control to the parents. Some of the greatest power struggles between parents and children really spring from the child's conviction: "Who are *you* to be telling me what to do?" Until that child is assured that we are offering a better way of life through our recovery, he'll continue to defy our authority as parents.

The successful resolution of control phase issues has to be worked out between husband and wife, parents and children. Parents *are* the rightful leaders of the family, and much of what contributes to healing during midphase recovery has to do with setting boundaries and limits for our children. As we move into the Affection Phase during ongoing recovery, we'll understand more about the child's need to have us take over the helm. Despite their fears, children really do want us to be responsible to them as leaders.

The Affection Phase

With the parent(s) at the helm as family leader, the family is able to become a closely knit group of people. The natural family role relationships have been restored. Parents get to be parents, and kids get to be kids. The giving and receiving of love is no longer threatening, for now it springs from a pure motive. When we no longer use our children to fulfill our needs inappropriately, we can offer our comfort and protection. Our guidance. Our support. Our love.

When we can begin to express love for our child, we have advanced a long way down the road of recovery.

But what happens when the Affection Phase runs its course? Think about your own experience. Recall a particularly close holiday or vacation time together. What usually follows? Family members will begin to distance and scatter briefly. Children may retreat with friends. One spouse may start working overtime at work. Another may retreat into some hobby or simply appear withdrawn and distant. Or, people outside the family may be sought for companionship, comfort, or advice. A sponsor's help may become suddenly more important than the marital partner. Extended family members may appear on the horizon.

Only so much intimacy is possible without the threat to our individual selfhood appearing as a resistance to closeness. That is why the Recovery Windmill has the smallest of the three blades as the Affection Phase. We need to keep in mind that the honeymoon doesn't last forever. But it can reappear, in a fresh form, given time and the slow but gradual circling of the Windmill back to the Affection Phase.

The Dynamic Law of the Recovery Windmill

And so, after the Affection Phase, we're swept back into the spaces of that Windmill again, caught up in another period of Family Relapse. The turbulence of this period is relative, depending on our resistance to it. If we "go with the flow" and allow family members to regroup naturally, the relapse period is brief. If we try to fight to recapture the old, comfortable period of the Affection Phase, we act against the natural rhythm and laws of the revolving Windmill.

After the relapse period, we're back into a new Inclusion Phase, where each family member questions again, "Just how much closeness do I really need? Or want? Do I want it from *this* family?"

This isn't dangerous thinking. It's normal and predictable, according to the dynamic law of the Recovery Windmill, which continues to recircle through a whole new course of Inclusion-Control-Affection phases.

The continuous revolving of the Recovery Windmill is inevitable. We needn't be alarmed by the changing reactions of our family members. The processes are as natural as the flow and force of the wind. We just need to remember to "go with the flow."

PART II

8 | The Stage of Family Life Called Recovery

Every family passes through normal and predictable stages of life: marriage, birth, child-rearing years, "empty nest syndrome," retirement, birth of grandchildren, and so on through the life cycle.

What I'm proposing now is that recovery is the beginning of a new family stage that brings an entirely new way of life. The old family drama, which spelled m-i-s-e-r-y through each of life's stages, is no longer relevant to the parent who relinquishes chemicals.

For the family in recovery is a brand new family. This may continue to sound strange since most of us believe that we at least know the people in our own families. However, the truth is that until recovery we scarcely know ourselves, let alone anyone else.

We are now ready to shift to this new stage of family life. There are no roles. There are no rules. And the plot has never been written. The play simply unfolds, one day at a time or, in this case, one ACT at a time.

This stage begins with three separate ACTs, which correspond to the three separate time zones in family recovery—early, middle, and long-term.

ACT is an acronym. This will serve as your memory key for the three most important healing principles that you will implement with your children. These principles correspond to the important *processes* during each of the three recovery phases; early, middle, and long-term recovery. We can designate these as ACT I, ACT II, and ACT III.

ACT I

ACT I reveals the family struggles of early recovery. The central process theme of ACT I is *belonging*. The important healing principles for parents to remember are:

*A*wareness

Commitment

Time

When we concentrate on using these principles in our relationships with our children, we will further not only their sense of really belonging to the family but also our own.

ACT II

Family membership begins to consolidate a year or so into recovery. By then you made your commitment as parents. Now you must work out the nature of your family relationships. Already you may have received some messages of hurt from your children as they became more trusting of your ability to parent them. But trust is still tinged with some fear. Resistance and power struggles emerge. The central process theme of ACT II is *control*. As parents learn to assume more and more of the leadership functions, healing will continue. During ACT II parents become increasingly active as leaders as you begin to:

Assert

Communicate

Teach

This stage is the midpoint in rebuilding relationships with your children.

ACT III

When control issues have been resolved, the rightful leadership of the family is restored to the parents. Husbands and wives now use the model of shared leadership. Or the single parent becomes the person of authority who assumes and delegates responsibilities for the children. The conflict resolution of ACT II actually paves the way for the emotional closeness that is experienced during ACT III. The central process theme of ACT III is the giving and receiving of affection—love. Three specific healing principles strengthen a family's ability to be more intimate during ACT III:

Affection

Consideration

Trust

This stage usually does not commence until long-term recovery.

The Acts of Healing

The word *heal* can be defined in terms of some very human undertakings. Yet the act of healing is often tinged with more mystical or supernatural associations. We rarely think of healing as an activity that we can carry out for ourselves and for our children. But successful recovery for each of us involves our active participation in the healing of our relationships, especially those with our children. The common pathway where chemical dependence leads us is the one to hurtful, distorted relationships with other people, particularly those closest to us.

We arrive at the end of this road feeling cut off from others, alone and depressed. Looking outwards in our confusion, we lay the blame on others. The memory of how others have disappointed and let us down lingers bitterly. We can see and feel our own hurt, but we remain blind to the emotional wounds of our children.

When we begin to think about healing the hurt of our children, many of us are like the members of the Parents in Recovery group. We feel inadequate. We look around for someone else to do the essential work for us. I want to allay your fears by explaining what I mean by healing.

I'm not proposing complicated psychological explanations. The simplest answers are usually the ones that ring most true. All you need to clarify my concept of healing is a dictionary.

> **Heal:** to become well or whole again; to restore the original purity or integrity; to restore (someone) to a healthy condition; to cause (painful) emotions to be no longer grievous.[8]

From Webster's, we learn that the word *heal* is a verb. A verb implies action. Healing will involve some action on your part. If we are talking about your healing, the actions you take will be in the service of your own recovery—to become well or whole again. If we are talking about healing of the parent-child relationship, we mean those actions that you can take to restore the original integrity of your relationship with your child.

No other motive in human relating is quite so pure as the original intent of a parent's love for a child. But somewhere along the addictive pathway, that original motive becomes distorted. The denial of chemical dependence blinds a parent to the child's needs. One of the most pressing needs of childhood is the right to live a chemically-free life.

We have no way as yet of knowing how the chemical use of a father or a mother leaves its impression on a child at the time of conception. But we do know that if a mother uses alcohol or other drugs during her prenatal period, these chemicals will disturb her child's delicate physical system.

When a child's infancy is marked by a parent's obsession with his or her own or with another's chemical use, then empathic caregiving is likely to be compromised. If any phase of a child's life is colored by the practice of chemical dependence in the family, then the child will have need of someone to guide him or her towards a healthier way of life. That someone is *you*. Your actions can foster healing in your children.

This book has been teaching that your child's most important resource for healing is you, the parent. You can see to it that your child's painful emotions are no longer grievous. This is what I mean by *healing the hurt*.

9 | Healing the Hurt— ACT I

"Healing. You make this first ACT sound so simple." Karra was reading the handout for the first class in the series. "*Awareness*. No problems there. I can *see* that my kids need help. *Commitment*. If I wasn't committed to my kids, I wouldn't be here, would I? But, *time*? You've got to be kidding. I announced at our first meeting that I'm stretched to my limit in recovery. Where am I supposed to find all this *extra* time? I'm a *single-parent*, remember?"

"Where did you get all that time from your kids when you were drinking and using?" Sam asked.

"I stole it!"

"Y'better believe we all steal time from our kids when we're drinking and drugging," Sara agreed.

"But we keep stealing time from them in recovery," Sam said to Sara. "Think about it, babe. While we were cleaning up our lives, Seth had to live in a foster home."

"Giving up time," Betsy reflected. "How do we do it? I'm like Karra, overextended already. And the fear's always there that if I don't keep working full-time, we'll go back on welfare."

"Well, I'm making a commitment to spend time with our kids," Chuck said.

"That's it!" Mimi said. "That's why *commitment* has to come before *time* in our ACTs of healing."

"And *awareness* before *commitment*, or we wouldn't even notice that our kids really need us," Chuck continued.

"Speaking of awareness," Karra observed, "I see a big definition being written across the board right now."

AWARENESS[8]

Consciousness of something or someone
when one allows it to enter his mind.
The application of acute sensitivity
to something or someone,
as intuition or sixth-sense.

Awake.

Alive.

Recovery is a journey of becoming more aware, more fully alive. Chemicals dull the senses and affect consciousness in ways that distort awareness. Eventually, chemicals contribute to heavy denial. You are hardly conscious of anything or anyone outside yourself. Whatever acute sensitivity you may have felt was merely a result of the varieties of chemically induced states you experienced. You weren't awake; you had become anesthetized by downers. Or, you were made hyper-alert to the point of paranoia by the drugs known as "uppers" or speed. Your chemical of choice altered your consciousness.

Children, on the other hand, are naturally aware. They are fully conscious, awake, and alive. They are painfully aware of some of the troubling memories of life with a chemically dependent parent. Sometimes they won't readily disclose this information, but they do retain the memory. (Think back to your own troubling childhood experiences. Can you still recall vividly some of your most traumatic times?)

It is from this same kind of trauma or hurt that your children will need healing.

ALIVE.
is to be
AWAKE
is to be
to be AWARE
RECOVERY.

Awareness is the first requirement of healing the hurt of your children. When you do not give in to the urge to close your eyes or to look away in denial, then you continue to move up the ladder of recovery and become more fully awake, aware, and alive.

You will learn to *see* again in recovery. When you first become aware of how chemical dependence has hurt your children, your natural tendency is to want to turn away.

Beyond this denial, which prevents your full awareness, is *fear. You don't want to see that you have repeated with your children that which was once done to you.* Like Karra and her looking-glass world, when what you see reflected back in the eyes of your children is your own childhood suffering, layers of hurt threaten to overwhelm.

You vowed that you would make a better way of life for your children. Yet you behaved selfishly or destructively without awareness of the harm to your own sons and daughters.

How can you possibly face up to the things you've said or done, many of which you may not even remember? How can you look into the eyes of your children, wondering what they have seen and heard? How can you possibly deal with the layers of hurt all at once?

Even in early recovery, you have the ability to face up to the painful emotions of your children. You can move through your own hurt to reach theirs.

Don't be surprised by your own resistance. Even as you're reading this page, you may find yourself rationalizing like Karra, "But I'm not sure that my children have been hurt by my chemical dependence." Or you may be tempted to minimize the harmful effects of your drinking and using. There are usually three negative emotions that prevent our awareness of our children's messages of hurt: fear, guilt, and shame. These feelings can lead us to hide behind a fortress of denial. But I am convinced that parents in recovery can move through their guilt and shame to compassion. To become aware, you need to do five things:

1. *Examine Your Original Motive.*

   Recall that you probably started out wanting to create a healthy way of life for your child. (You certainly intended to do better by your children than had been done to you.) Even if you grew up in the best of homes, as did Sam and Sara, something important was missing. You didn't feel loved and valued for yourself. Somewhere along the way you turned to chemicals as a way of compensating. Tragically, your parenting commitment was lost to chemicals. Both *you* and your child were lost to this tragedy. ACT I is about beginning a parallel course of recovery with your child.

2. *Ask For Help.*

   To maintain the clear, bright focus of awareness, you're going to need some help. Chemicals continue to maintain denial for several months into recovery. Let me offer some suggestions. In the early stage of recovery, find a helper—such as a sponsor, a counselor, or a trusted friend in recovery. Or think about starting or joining a Parents in Recovery group. We need other people to serve as our eyes and ears during this early phase of recovery.

Remember that the forces of chemical dependence and co-dependence lead to problems in perception. You'll often misperceive the motives or actions of others, especially your children. Sometimes you'll feel totally confused by them. Often you overreact and say or do things that are reminiscent of the old dysfunctional days before recovery. For a while into recovery, you may not even trust your spouse to provide you with accurate information about your interactions with your children.

When you set about to find a sponsor or a counselor, keep in mind that you're going to need someone who has a sincere interest in helping you through this journey of family recovery. If a prospective helper tends to minimize your children's hurt, then recognize that this is an individual who may have some personal blind spots. Beware of the helper who speaks with the voice of denial in helping you appraise the past, such as telling you that "You did the best you could." No one does his or her *best* under the influence of chemicals or denial. *Recovery is about increasing awareness and getting rid of denial.*

3. *Start a Journal.*

    A daily journal can sharpen your awareness. This is also an important tool of therapy not only for improving mental health but also to help improve physical well-being. (Did you know that the immune system has been found to be strengthened by journal writing? Research has shown that after journal writing stopped, the immune system continued to be improved for six months thereafter.)

    If you face your journal honestly, you are moving out of denial into awareness. Awareness and health go hand in hand. Awareness is being more fully alive!

    When you are involved in journal writing, you can ventilate some of your most destructive thoughts and feelings without ever bringing harm to your child—or to anyone else for that matter! During times when a sponsor or a counselor is unavailable to help you sort through this conflict with your child, use your journal as a sounding board. You may express four letter words (if that's what it takes) or say unkind things about your child or spouse (if that's what you're thinking). You can talk about what an ungrateful child you have who doesn't appreciate all that you're doing to recover. (Because sometimes you probably will feel this way in a weak moment of self-pity.) You can expose your angry, bitter, self-pitying emotions to your journal. You can wallow in these feelings, enjoy them, and then let them go! Give them to the journal and then put that aside for a while. Later, you may decide to review what you wrote with a sponsor or counselor who can help you develop even greater awareness into some of your strong reactions to your child. These journal entries will come to be your most valuable therapeutic tool in early recovery. Can you see what has been healing about this process?

First, you have discharged all your negative, hostile emotions towards a little child, *but you didn't actually say or do anything to hurt the child*. Unlike times when you were drinking or using other drugs and were prone to lash out at your child with hurtful words, *this time* you didn't! (Remember, cruel words *spoken* are as difficult to replace as getting toothpaste back into the tube!) With the cruel words written, you can retract them. You can rip out the whole page of angry words, if necessary, and then forget about them—forever. When you release pent-up feelings of frustration to your journal, you will be all the more likely to increase your awareness of the source of your overreaction. You will also gain more awareness of your child's part in the conflict. Remember that today's source of rage may be tomorrow's blessing.

I do want to encourage that this journal writing be done out of the child's presence. Particularly when you are using the journal to deal with harsh anger towards your child, try to find a journal "retreat," such as another room. You do not want to increase your child's self-consciousness by letting him know that you are writing about him. (He will come to hate your journal!) And you certainly want to refrain from laying guilt on your child by saying, "You've made me so angry that I have to go lock myself in my room to write about you." Above all, you do not want your child to feel guilty or resentful about your journal entries.

Journal use in early recovery is a valuable tool for learning to be more aware of your children as individuals. As you write about frustrating interactions with a child, you may not be seeing clearly as you write. After a couple of days, when you go back to what you have written, you will find that you have increased awareness into your child and yourself. What formerly had bewildered you now becomes clear. Your journal becomes your therapist, helping you develop insight and understanding.

Awareness is the route to becoming more fully centered in the present. You want to rid your children and yourself from the grudges and resentments of the past. Awareness will help you let go of these ghosts of the past and begin to see present-day relationships more clearly. The noise inside your mind, which is full of preconceived notions and judgments, will gradually lessen.

4. *Expand Your Awareness.*

    This is an exercise that you can put into practice right away to increase your awareness: Take an unfamiliar route to work, to a meeting, to the supermarket, or to another part of town. Whether you walk, drive, or take the bus, note your reactions and impressions. Later, contrast these with your awareness as you travel the same old familiar route.

    When we are faced with newness and unfamiliarity, we have sharpened our perceptions and awarenesses. We are literally seeing the world through the eyes of a child, in a fresh, new way. This is in contrast to our way of proceeding with the mundane or familiar. Much of what we see is distorted by our preconceived notions and inner judgments of what we think we *will* see, based on our experiences of the past. (Expectations from the past narrow the focus of our awareness.)

When you expand your awareness of your new family in recovery and your children, you concentrate on observing the moment-by-moment unfolding of the journey. Contrast this to times when you try to stage-direct your family. When you begin to play *your* role mechanically, you also stop knowing yourself. The same old troubled patterns will take over, and you will not know how to end the play. (Life becomes unmanageable!)

With expanding awareness, you merely observe the play as it develops spontaneously and effortlessly, according to the natural processes of family reorganization. Now, the world of your family becomes interesting to you. You are no longer on the sidelines, nor are you in the director's chair. You are a part of your own experience, moment by moment. Expanding your awareness in this way really is an art.

5. *Stop, Look, and Listen!*

   As you develop the art of awareness, remember that your child also has a head full of negative images from the past. It's important to keep your child centered more fully in the present, but you'll also need to attend to those messages of hurt that a child continues to repeat. A past traumatic memory will be reworked by the child like a broken record either through his comments to you or through his behavior.

   How can you keep your child centered in the present, fully aware of the parent who you are today, and still attend to the painful repetitions from the past, as well as heal him for tomorrow? Stop, look, and listen!

   Too often parents, or even counselors, rush in and tell a child that the past is over. But for that child, the past *isn't* over until her painful memories have stopped. When you hear a child repeating information about what happened when you were drinking and using, you need to *stop*. Yes, that's right, stop whatever you're doing. *Look*, by making eye contact with your child so that you keep her centered with you in the here and now. Then, *listen*.

Listen to what she says with your full attention so that you will be able to reassure her as she *relives* her hurt. Because that *is* what's happening. The repetitive story or behavior means that a child is continuing to be tormented in the present by the past. When you, as the sober, recovering parent, *join* your child—however briefly—she is reassured by your comfort and your presence. You can then use words like the following to strengthen this act of healing:

> Life didn't feel very safe for you when Mommy and Daddy were drinking and drugging and always fighting. You didn't have anyone to help you, and you were scared and angry inside. But *today* you're safe. You can come to us anytime you need to talk to us about what happened back then. We don't use chemicals anymore. We want you to feel protected and loved by us.

When a youngster is gently reminded of the present-day reality, she eventually begins to see you in a new and different way. She begins to react differently towards you. Your child's new, inner images lead her to greater self-acceptance as she forms more positive identifications with you. She will want to be like the parent she knows in recovery rather than the destructive parent she used to fear.

When you assist your child to move out of the past, she can choose new, healthier behaviors for the future. For example, I suggested to Sara that she and Sam could begin to work with Seth's current eating problem by the *Stop, Look, and Listen!* technique. By bringing Seth gently back into the present, Sara could help heal his hurt and help him change his own behavior for the future. She would begin by acknowledging the message of hurt in the following way:

> Seth, I know that I must have caused you to feel very confused back when we were using drugs. I was wrong to worry you about food by always harping on you to save some for later. Your dad and I are making

sure now that you always have enough to eat, so *you* don't have to worry. We're going to take care of you. I can see that you're still afraid, sometimes. After a while you won't be afraid anymore, and then you won't need to take food away from the table with you.

When you leave the child with a *positive suggestion* at the end, you are placing confidence in his ability to heal. We each have this remarkable capacity to heal, and the reassurance of another strengthens and supports us.

As we go forward in healing the hurt of our children, we'll come to the place where we need to make a *commitment*.

COMMITMENT[8]

Something which engages one to do something.
A continuous obligation.

A promise.

A pledge.

Your awareness of your child's hurt must be followed by your conscious decision to improve the quality of your relationship with this child. The commitment is your renewed vow, your promise, and your pledge to carry the decision forward.

A commitment to your child's healing requires that you must do something. ACTion must be taken. But first, a word of caution: *You are not expected to change your child's life for the better in a few days or even a few weeks or months.* Remember the Recovery Windmill? The processes of family recovery never stop happening. The Windmill continues to revolve, pushing you toward greater levels of growth and healing. Those who expect immediate change run the risk of being disillusioned. Worse, you may begin to pressure a child who already has been severely stressed.

The journey of shared recovery between parent and child is ongoing, without a particular destination. The journey of recovery *is* the destination. You already have embarked. Now, you are making sure that your children are traveling alongside you.

Words of Commitment

When Karra needed help with knowing just how to put her commitment into words for her children, this is what I suggested that she might say:

> Angel, Billy, or Sandy (said to each child *individually*), I'm aware that you were hurt and scared by my drinking and drug use. I don't know what you remember about that time that still bothers you, but we can talk about it anytime you want or need to. You're not going to hurt my feelings or make me angry. I know you may even hate me for some of the things that I said or did to you when I was drinking and using. It's even OK to tell me about that, because I hated some of the things I did and said to hurt you. I know that I was wrong. I'm very, very sorry. And I'm trying in recovery to make sure that I never hurt you in that way again.

One or more of your children may ask if you're ever going to drink or use other drugs again. Beware of making "never, never" promises such as "I'm never, never going to drink or use again for as long as I live." Simply reassure your child gently that *he or she* doesn't have to worry about your problem. Explain briefly about your program of recovery. Your words of commitment will be honest and realistic ones about the program of recovery that is helping you maintain sobriety or abstinence.

Written Words

You may want to write out a more detailed commitment in your journal just for yourself as it pertains to your children. Later you may want to review this with your sponsor or counselor. For an older child, you can even use the written form to communicate your commitment. However, when you give it to the child, use the *Stop, Look, and Listen!* technique. Read the words aloud. Share the moment. Of course, with an adult child who is removed by time and distance, you may want to mail a letter and discuss it later over the telephone.

Your commitment to healing the hurt of your children is one of the most important keys to successful parent-child recovery.

Levels of Commitment

When a couple who is having relationship problems comes to me for assistance, one of the first assessments that I make has to do with the nature of their commitment. Even for a couple who has been married for twenty years or more, there often was never a genuine commitment. (Recall that a commitment is a promise or a pledge of *continuous* obligation to each other.) The members of a couple will be able to tell me in great detail about how they do not feel supported by each other, about how they live parallel but separate lives, and about how their efforts to sabotage each other are succeeding.

Usually the couple has been stuck at the level of the *Inclusion Phase* of family processes, continuing to question with ambivalence whether or not they should even be together in the first place. If I ask them, "When you began your relationship, how did you go about making a commitment?" they stare at me blankly.

"Commitment?"

Most of the time a commitment wasn't made. Although a couple may have repeated marriage vows, they parroted the empty commitment of meaningless words that really didn't hold any significance. "... 'Til death do us part" loses its meaning almost overnight when a couple has a low tolerance for the disillusionment, the frustrations, and the challenges of family life.

Many modern couples enter into serial relationships, no better prepared for the next than they were for the first, never offering an authentic commitment. Those of you who have grown up in chemically dependent families literally *fear* commitment. You're not sure that you want to commit to any one or any group. Behind this fear is the even greater fear of closeness. Like Fred, you may feel that if you don't come up for air, you'll lose your selfhood to the family.

But a family without commitment can't become a cohesive, safe, and intimate haven. The hard work of commitment begins between husband and wife and is then made parent to parent for the preservation of the family as a group. But here I want to offer the following words of caution from *The Self in the System*, written by Dr. Michael P. Nichols:[9]

> Common sense tells us that, though you are joined together with others, you are still separate persons. If you do not give heed to the (separate) *selves* that make up families, you miss the reality of those you seek to help and you lose the leverage necessary to make them *partners* in a *joint endeavor*. (Italics mine.)

The joint endeavor that you're considering here is the commitment between parent and child. Dr. Nichols, a specialist in family therapy, tells us in the quote above that for the commitment to succeed, you'll need to form a *partnership* with that child. Yet, the solid observations and wisdom of the founding fathers of Alcoholics Anonymous describe the great difficulty in forming a partnership:

> The primary fact that you fail to recognize is your total inability to form a true *partnership* relationship with another human being. Your egomania digs two disastrous pitfalls. Either you insist upon dominating the people you know (including children), or you depend upon them far too much.[10]

Practically speaking, you can't enter into a committed relationship, or partnership, with anyone until you acknowledge the unique and special qualities of that individual. This is never more true than with children.

It is important to keep in mind that I do not mean physical caretaking such as feeding, clothing, etc., but rather the capacity of the parents to perceive the *unique characteristics* of the child's emerging *self* and to respond to these in a positive, supportive manner, to identify, acknowledge, and treat with respect his or her unique temperament . . . to encourage his unique style or manner . . . in his exploring, experimenting, self-assertive adventures with reality.[11]

TIME[8]

A period during which a certain action is taken
(Early recovery is the time to
begin to heal the hurt of your children);

A period set apart in some way
(The early stage of recovery
can be thought of as ACT I);

A favorable period
(Now is the time to begin to heal the hurt);

Leisure; opportunity
(I will take more time with
my children during recovery);

A definite moment of the hour or day
(I can devote the evening hours to my children).

Time seems to be a perplexing standard of measure for parents in recovery. Time distortions plague us. B/R, the time period *before recovery* that you know as "the past," continues to haunt us. The years of the past may seem collapsed into the smallest unit of time. D/R, the time period *during recovery,* seems to lag by comparison. Getting through twenty-four hours is difficult sometimes. Each minute of an hour can also seem interminable when it is the time between drinks or pills or a fix—whatever your drug of choice.

You count the days of your abstinence over and over, watching the days stretch into a week, or a month, or ninety days, ever so slowly.

Then, suddenly, time begins to speed up. You always seem to be playing catch-up. A couple of parenting responsibilities tacked onto a hurried conversation with your children may seem sufficient until you realize that healing the hurt requires you to STOP.

You must begin to make time and to take time for your children. How is this possible when personal recovery demands so much? Like Karra, you may ask "Where am I supposed to find all this TIME?"

Remember, in the first ACT of healing, before *time* comes *commitment.* Are there commitments that you need to review before beginning to develop quality time for your children? Is a life-style change necessary? *You* must be the judge of that. But as you review your present commitment, you may want to look back over one twenty-four hour period. Then examine a week and even a month of commitments. Beware of commitments that do not result in lasting or long-term payoffs. An empty night of television viewing. Too much time spent on the telephone. Sleep time and even eating time can be reviewed. What about the time spent cleaning? (We can become fanatics about cleanliness in recovery!) What about shopping? If you're a shopaholic, think about a lifestyle change in this area. Trim your budget and rearrange your schedule at the same time. *Can you unselfishly and willingly begin to surrender little blocks of time to your children?*

To surrender time to a child *is in and of itself an act of healing.* But quality time spent with a child means that you are present for that child. If you had little quality time from a parent during your own childhood, you may find the greatest internal struggle as you try to

123

make time for your child. You'll experience vague annoyance. You may feel impatient or bored. Your own lonely, unnoticed child is screaming out in rebellion, "What about ME? I need some time for Me." So, your mind will wander to all those legitimate needs of recovery (meetings, aftercare, counseling, etc.) or to household tasks (cleaning, shopping, or watering the lawn). Anytime you find this happening, tell yourself, "STOP!" Ask if any of these activities is truly more important at this exact moment than the time you've set aside for your child.

The most important question that you can ask silently as you are with your child is "Who are you?" Allow your child to teach you.

Quality rather than quantity of time is the key. If you feel uncomfortable at first by spending time with your child, then make a commitment to set aside distinct time intervals. Use small amounts of time at first, such as twenty minutes or so, to lavish your child with attention. Suggest that the two of you play a board game. (Children love board games!) This time spent together, just the two of you, will begin to open up your awareness and provide the answer to the question "Who are you?" Observe how the child challenges and strategizes to win the game. Let him tell you with words or actions just why it's so important for him to win. See what he does in the face of frustration. How does he experience failure? How does he plan and anticipate?

Other quality times at home can be spent in an activity such as art work: painting, pasting, coloring, building, etc. Do a project together. Build a birdhouse. Do a science experiment. Let the child help you plan just how to spend the twenty-minute time period. Before you know it, you'll be *enjoying* yourself, and the time will have extended longer than you thought.

You can also plan special Saturday or Sunday afternoon outings. I suggested to Karra that she might want to designate one Saturday afternoon for each of her three children and the fourth one for herself.

Allow your child to help plan the activity for the outing: a play, a puppet show, a picnic, the zoo, the park, and so on. Older children may ask you to take them shopping. Beware! Allow them the freedom to make their own choices within your budget constraints. The point is this—teens may or may not want your advice. Even if they ask for your opinion, don't blurt out your *true* opinion: "That skirt is the ugliest thing I've ever seen!" You don't have to lie or fabricate an answer. You can respond simply, "I can see that the skirt really pleases you, and that you want it." But teens also try to bait us. So, don't be surprised if your child says, "Oh, so *you* don't like it? Why didn't you just say so!" In cases like this, what do you do? Go with the flow. Don't become frustrated over the entrapment. *Remember, this child is teaching you about WHO she is.* She has just informed you that: (1) She's still shaky in her self-confidence; (2) She doesn't trust her own opinions; (3) She doesn't really want yours either; and (4) Life is complex for this unsettled fourteen-year-old. (Didn't we all feel that way at one time or another—never quite trusting our parents because they weren't "hip," yet lacking confidence in our own decisions?) While your teen is going through her confusion, remember the mission and the question that you're continuing to repeat silently to yourself: "Who are you?" Don't even think of this time as yours. Think of it as *hers.* You're surrendering time freely and unselfishly, releasing time from your busy recovery schedule and the rest of your life to be with this very important person in your life—your child.

Parents may not realize the importance of simply *being* with a child—of spending time as an act of healing.

But this may be the very first time that you've made yourself available to your child.

Simply being with a child is one of the most important therapeutic aspects in the psychotherapy of children. Being with the child as he or she talks or plays and you listen or observe or participate as directed is the cornerstone of healing in child-centered therapy.

Consider yourself a student of child development for whatever period of time that you are able to set aside. Learn about WHO this child in your presence really is. Attune yourself to the child's inner self, beyond and between the words that are spoken. Try to catch a glimpse of the wonderful human being that is your child. As you attune yourself more sensitively through the art of awareness, you'll be involved in the process of *empathic attunement*. Your sixth sense will lead you to your child's inner world.

Empathic Attunement

With empathic attunement, you're providing *feedback*. You're letting the child know that you know what it's like to be him. The little kid says, "I feel *real*." The older child says, "I feel *understood*." Your *feedback* that you know what it is like to be in your child's world helps fill up the emptiness of his lonely unnoticed self.

Empathic attunement is not the same as what some folks call "focused attention." During the latter, we seem to occupy an external *role* that is often experienced by the child as prying or meddling. Focused attention without feedback can simply be prying or meddling as it is experienced by a child. Even our gaze or presence will seem an intrusion. In the face of our intrusiveness, the people-pleasing child may dismiss her own needs altogether and try to *feed back* to us exactly what she thinks we want and need to hear.

With empathic attunement, you concentrate your observations on the unspoken messages that the child will send through such subtle communications as a gesture, a shrug, or an inquiring glance. You always remain at a respectful distance, yet close enough to take your lead from the child, to sense her readiness, and to participate as you are beckoned. The little child needs to feel no more intrusion than your supportive presence, should she desire to make use of it.

10 | Healing the Hurt— ACT II

"I'm noticing changes with the kids—some I'm not sure I like," Fred began. "I've practiced those ideas from our classes last month, but I still don't know how to be the kind of father who stands up to his kids the right way."

"Yes, he's a regular Disneyland Dad," Mimi said. "And since I've given up control, the kids run the show."

"Mimi gets a lot of back talk from the girls these days," Fred explained.

"Welcome to the club! My Angel is mouthy, but I just keep telling myself, 'It's a message of hurt. *A message of hurt.'*" Karra said.

"And Sassy's back to her old self, sassier than ever now that I've moved back home. My boy-twin keeps quiet, but he sure looks daggers at me. Our older kids seem to resent the life outa both Bitsy and me."

"Seth's more strong-willed," Sam said. "But I'm glad to see the kid finally coming out of his slump."

"That's easy for you to say!" Sara retorted. "You don't have to wrestle with him every morning to get him off to school."

"So? You want me to give up my job and stay home and help?"

"You threatening me with the streets again, Sam? The kid's getting more like you every day. Stubborn. I could use a little support, y'know?"

"Hey. First time I ever heard you kids argue," Chuck smiled.

"What's that question that's supposed to come up in ACT II?" Karra asked. "Isn't it, 'Who's in charge of this family?' I'd say we're all ready to start learning more about that."

ASSERT[8]

Assert
To make effective. To maintain. To insist on.

Assert oneself
To become active. To impose one's proper authority.

Assertion
A positive statement.

Assert is from the Latin word *asserere*, which literally means to "claim or set free a slave by laying one's hand on his head." The act of healing also has been associated with the laying on of hands. Certainly, during this phase of healing, you are going to want to "claim or set free" your children who may have become slaves to the type of family dysfunction that existed before your recovery. Children may have carried on parenting roles for their brothers and sisters, and one child may have functioned as a type of pseudo-parent to you or to your spouse. Having become aware of these troubled family patterns, you are now ready to initiate actions that foster change.

Restoring Family Leadership

Leadership is one of the functions that parents commonly relinquish when they progress in their chemical dependence. Just as Fred gave up control to Mimi, it is not unlikely that you gave up leadership to your spouse or even to one or more of your children. Recall from our discussion on family processes that leadership is a *function*. Whoever is carrying out this function at any point in time is serving as the leader of the group, organization, or family.

Now, during this middle phase of recovery, you are being asked to assert yourself as the rightful leader of the family, to "impose your proper authority" by again assuming a parental control. Like the members of the Parents in Recovery group, you can expect resistance from your children through power struggles and acts of defiance or subtle manipulation.

The Control Continuum

We cannot talk about the middle phase of family recovery without calling attention to that seemingly evil word, *control*. Few of us want to admit to a basic need for control. We've heard so many negative associations to the word. Yet psychologist W.C. Schutz tells us that control is one of *three basic human needs*. Next, after a sense of attachment and belonging, we have a basic desire for a sense of mastery and control over our lives.

> Control behavior refers to the decision-making process between people, and the areas of power, influence and authority. The need for control varies along a continuum from the desire for power, authority and control over others (and therefore over one's own future) to the need to be controlled and have responsibility lifted from oneself.[6]

Below is a graphic representation of what I believe Schutz may be talking about in terms of a control continuum:

	Democratic	
DOMINANCE	Leadership	DEPENDENCE
desire for power and total authority over the child		desire for all responsibility to be lifted
(Parent)		(Infant)

During infancy, parents need to assume total authority over the totally dependent child. However, as the child grows and matures, parental dominance decreases. At the midpoint of the continuum the democratic leader or parent teaches and guides by example or by role modeling. The area of overlap in the center indicates child-centered or empathic parenting, when the parent considers the needs and rights of the child's position but also recognizes the child's need for guidance and limits. Both the parent's and the child's positions fluctuate on the continuum according to the age of the child. As the child enters adolescence, parenting responsibilities lessen considerably as the teenager makes bids for personal autonomy.

We've already discussed in ACT I the problems that chemically dependent parents have in recovery. Karra leaned on Angel heavily during her drinking and using period. In recovery she went to the other extreme on the control continuum, trying to dominate. Mimi's problem in parenting was just the reverse of Karra's. Overly controlling while Fred was drinking, Mimi saw recovery as an opportunity for Fred to share leadership. She moved to the right of continuum. Fred was at the far right of the continuum during both his drinking period and early phase of recovery. Now, although he is moving slightly more to the left, he and Mimi seem caught in that overlap position of a *power vacuum* where neither is asserting effective leadership.

Sam tells us that Seth's strong will is positive. Sara disagrees. For the first time, this family appears caught up in a *power struggle* as a result of the changes in their child during recovery.

During this phase of recovery as you go about parenting your children, you may want to check your position on the control continuum and ask yourself if you are being domineering without regard for their self-needs. If you tell your teenager how to wear his hair and how to think, act, and speak, you're probably too far to the left on the continuum. On the other hand, if you permit your children to abuse you, to be disrespectful, or to openly defy important health and safety rules, then you have probably opted out of the family and moved too far to the right on the continuum.

When both parents relinquish their rightful positions as leaders of the family, chaos results. Or, in Chuck's words, "All hell breaks loose." When Betsy called Chuck back into the family, he had to move to the far left of the control continuum for a brief period until his teenagers began treatment. Although parents need to be flexible, moving from the position of dominance during infancy, to a midpoint as the child matures, and to a lessening of control during the teen years, they always have a responsibility to protect their children from self-destructive practices.

Control issues will emerge spontaneously within your family, whether you like it or not, as you progress in recovery. Your renewed commitment initially has a disorganizing effect on your children. They tend to resent your leadership because they don't trust you to grant them a better way of life. Also, their unhealed hurts from the past are starting to get closer to the surface as they do start to trust you. This is the time when those *messages of hurt* become loud and clear. Listen to your child's cries—not often through words but through defiance, rebellion, resentment, power struggles, back talk, testing of limits, and yes, attempts to sabotage your leadership. Sometimes it may even seem to you that your child is trying to sabotage your recovery.

Your children are not consciously aware of what they are doing or why, as they send messages of hurt. If you remain steadfast, you can help reassure them that you are strong enough to cope with their hurt.

Shared Leadership

In two-parent families, bids for dominance and control seem to occur as power struggles. Sam and Sara are a case in point. The tight, co-dependent bond between them is loosening as their son, Seth, grows stronger in recovery. Sam supports his son's changes as positive, but Sara is feeling unsupported and at odds with both her husband and her son. This is the phase of recovery when family tempers flare and no one wants to budge an inch towards compromise. Troubled marriages can result from this period unless parents learn to share leadership functions. With the exception of Karra, who is a single parent, each of the families in the Parents in Recovery group need to use a shared leadership model.

To implement this model with your family, it's important to begin to educate your children about the laws that govern family functioning. Hold a family meeting and explain this notion of leadership. Here's an example of what Chuck and Betsy explained to their children:

> Your mom and I are trying to learn to work together as a team to be the leaders in this family. We never learned from our folks, but we're going to meetings and classes and we're learning now. We've also learned from our mistakes. Your mom worked too much away from home, and I drank too much when I did come home, so you kids didn't have any leadership. But that's all going to change.

By now younger children may start to fidget and become restless. Teens may sit and glare in defiance. Recognize these resistances as your children's internal struggles. *They're not really convinced that you know how to lead them.*

So, begin to explain leadership. Tell your children that every group or organization must have a leader—someone in charge—for things to run smoothly. Draw attention to the president, the governor, and other civic leaders. For younger children, you can illustrate the idea of shared leadership by referring to the school. (Every child understands the concept of a "boss.") You can ask, "Who is the boss or leader at school?" Sometimes a child will answer teacher *or* principal or sometimes teacher *and* principal. You can explain that in school the teacher *and* the principal are co-leaders. And at home, the mother *and* the father are co-leaders. Most young children in recovery will now be sitting with rapt attention as you present this new format. It makes sense. (Of course, this is what they have wanted all along. Children *want* and *need* to be able to lean on their parents.)

With your adolescent children, you may encounter some very different reactions, depending on the amount of sealed-over hurt that they are expressing as defiance and resentment. But even the most hostile, self-destructive teen may surprise you. A few days after I've helped parents intervene and assist their chemically dependent teen into treatment, I've heard that youngster say to the parents, "I'm glad you did it. I know that you *care.*"

All children need limit setting from their parents. Yet, we may have learned as young parents or as young teenagers that children need to "do their own thing." Many of us who grew up in the era of permissiveness tend to carry these attitudes into our parenting. In recovery a child who defies your first tentative gestures at establishing rules can intimidate you.

Shared parenting presents a problem when a mother and a father disagree with one another on a given family rule. There is no *easy* way out of the conflict that's likely to result. You need to work *through* the conflict and come up with a *consensus*: something that both parents can live with and something that will help the overall functioning of your family.

Rules and Requests

An important distinction needs to be made for children when the notion of family "rules" and "requests" is presented. You may begin by explaining to your children that they developed some very confusing

133

rules during the time that you were drinking and using. Ask your children to talk about some of these rules:

> "Tiptoe down the hall so you don't wake Daddy when he's hung over."

> "When Mom passes out on the couch, make sure her cigarette is not left burning in the ashtray."

> "Don't tell Grandma when Mom stays out all night."

> "Get out of the house when Mom and Dad are fighting."

Ask the children to share with you some of the other "rules" that they had to create during your family's troubled times. Then explain that your family needs new rules based on the principles of a better way of life.

Next, discuss some of the more functional rules that children already know from school, church, scouting, or sports. Then explain that your recovering family needs a whole new set of "good rules." You may say that your recovery is leading you to improved parenting and that the new rules will help the children understand your new expectations, such as the time they must come home from school, the time they must set aside for homework, and the time they must devote to chores and other responsibilities.

You can then make a distinction about "requests," explaining that your child may make a "request" of a parent for some special privilege. However, a child may not break a parent's rule on a whim. A child may "request" that a rule be changed; but if the child breaks a rule without prior permission, consequences will occur.

Consequences

"What happens if a kid forgets and breaks a rule?" your child may ask either innocently or shrewdly, perhaps looking for a loophole.

You need to explain the idea of *consequences*, or something that your child can expect to follow both desirable and undesirable rule behavior. However, assure your child that you're going to be working with him to help him remember as you *teach* him the new family rules.

You can award a star or points—depending on the age of the child—each time that he complies with a rule. He can earn bonus points for exceeding expectations. If you expect him home at four o'clock when school is out at three, tell him that he can earn a gold star for coming home by three-thirty or a silver star by coming home on time. You can discuss with your child what he would like to choose as a reward when he earns a certain number of silver or gold stars (or points) at the end of each week. He may choose to do something such as go on a family outing. Or you may allow your teenager to go on a date or have use of the family car for a special occasion.

Your older child may look down his nose at the star method, but you can keep a behavioral chart in some other way. Keeping the chart visible for the entire family to see provides positive feedback from others about the child's progress.

I can't overemphasize the importance of spending time with your child while going over the consequences for desired or undesirable behaviors. After the goal behavior has been established and you have discussed the consequences, have the child repeat back the behavior and the consequences—both positive and negative. In two-parent families, mother and father will need to agree on the goal and the consequences.

Don't be surprised if you, your spouse, or a particular child have to continue to review a particular goal behavior and each person's understanding of the original negotiation. This is particularly necessary when a child has been in the position of family leader where one simple behavior may need discussing over and over for several weeks at a time. If this seems redundant and a waste of time, keep in mind that a *family process* is occurring that actually has to do with three simultaneous events:

1. the child's ebb and flow in accepting and rejecting your leadership,

2. the power struggle that exists between you and your spouse as you attempt to refine the shared leadership model, and

3. the tendency for the three of you to slide back into a period of family relapse where you wonder if you even want to be a part of the family.

For example, Sam and Sara agreed that Seth's problem with dawdling in the morning was presenting a problem for the family. Sam ignored the behavior, seeing it as Sara's responsibility to get Seth ready for school. Sam was the breadwinner in the family, and he saw his responsibility as getting himself off to work. He wasn't supporting Sara as she tried to implement more healthy behaviors for Seth. Sam believed that Sara was trying to suck him into her daily morning arguments with Seth. He felt entitled to go off to his job feeling calm and serene.

After the class on shared leadership, Sam agreed to support Sara by discussing the problem with Seth. Together they told Seth that he was no longer permitted to watch television in the morning or to play in his room before school. Only after Seth had finished breakfast and dressed for school was he permitted to play, if time allowed. (While this may sound like a simple enough family rule, several weeks actually passed before Seth became responsible in his pre-school behavior.)

Assertion of Positive Statements

The final meaning associated with the verb *assert* has to do with asserting positive statements. A parent's affirmations to a child go a long way towards strengthening that child's sense of self. Does it seem odd that I'm suggesting that you need to *strengthen* your child during this period when control issues and power struggles are occurring? When a child's self-esteem improves and he begins to develop a feeling of inner worth and value, that child will more readily accept your rules and limits.

Remember that negative interactions are so much a part of chemically dependent family life that they become deeply ingrained habit patterns for you and for your children. Life has been spent in the negative lane where even your affection was tinged with sarcasm or teasing. Recall some of Chuck's cruel statements to his boy-twin when the boy displayed his artistic talent. Even though Chuck recognized the boy's "fantastic little drawing" as special, he would not praise his child. Instead he teased and ridiculed him. He shamed the boy. Karra, too, used bitter, rejecting words to Billy when she spoke to him under the influence of her nightly vodka.

All your negative programming affects the way a child thinks and feels abut who he is. Your words and actions have a direct bearing on your child's inner self-experience. We can use words to build up and enhance a child's self-confidence or to cut him down and emotionally batter him. Chuck could have said, "Wow, son! I'm proud of you. That's a fantastic drawing!" These words would have cost him little, but they would have provided his son with a treasure of praise to cherish and remember. Positive words that are never spoken can be as harmful to a child as hostile criticism. The lonely, unnoticed self of a little child cries out for praise.

Sometimes we may think that we're praising, but the positive statement is diluted by our veiled criticism: "Johnny is usually so helpful and considerate with his school chums—I wonder why he can't be that way with his brothers and sisters." Your child's inner world, his sense of who he is, is channeled through these negative statements.

You cancel out the praise you give for Johnny's helpfulness and consideration with his school chums by highlighting his deficiency. Johnny is left with the impression that no matter how good he is, he is never quite good enough.

An Experiment with Your Child's Inner World

Let's try an experiment. Have someone look down on you while standing over you on a stepstool or a low chair. Now have that person lavish you with positive words. As you hear the words, concentrate on your inner *experience*. Listen to your body's wisdom as your muscles relax, your tension decreases, and you feel buoyed up. Then have the person switch to negative faultfinding, to critical words spoken in a loud or punitive manner, or to sharp words that tell you what you should do to be more acceptable. Again, listen to your body's wisdom. Then contrast your experience. What did this experiment teach you about being a child?

Even the consequences for undesirable behavior or for a restriction can be stated in a positive way:

> Instead of saying,
>
> "Mary, you are a thief for stealing money from your brother. You are going to have to be punished."
>
> You can say,
>
> "Mary, you will need to do your brother's chores for the next week to repay the money that you took without asking."

In the first statement, you denounced Mary by calling her a thief and threatening some unstructured but frightening punishment. In the second statement, straightforward yet considerate, you simply state the actual punishment and say what Mary has done without criticizing and labeling her. You may want to use your journal to help you retranslate some of your negative feelings and attitudes into positive assertions for your child.

COMMUNICATE[8]

To give or pass on information.

To make others understand one's ideas.

To be in touch by words or signals.

To be joined by a common door, gate, etc.

138

Most of us have experienced some type of communication problem in the past. This is one of the most frequent problems I hear expressed when people are first seeking counseling. When I ask for more specifics about these problems in communication, the descriptions may be blurred and vague. Until asked to sort through our communication failures, most of us think that the other person is the one causing the problem.

Consider the different meanings implied in the verb *communicate*. Children from chemically dependent families experience numerous problems in verbal as well as in nonverbal communication. This inability to communicate contributes to problems in school, with peers, and at home. Moreover, your children seem to pick up the faulty communication styles that you have used when you were under the influence of chemicals, when you were sobering up, as well as when you were in recovery. Many of these communications consist of negative, critical, or fault-finding interactions. Children learn sarcasm, harsh put-downs, and other forms of verbal warfare from parents. They repeat these negative communications during their sibling and peer interactions. We tend to expose our children to a lot of talk but very little actual information, understanding, or empathic joining. When you begin to provide sensitive, positive comments to your child about his wants and needs, you have joined him through empathy.

Troubled Communication Patterns

One woman who clarified negative communication patterns in families was Virginia Satir (often referred to as "the mother of family therapy"). Satir identified four types of communication patterns that are related to low self-esteem.[12] Not only do these patterns produce a negative effect on the self-experience of the child, but also they interfere with the parent-child relationship by increasing the child's fear and dependency. Satir believed that these patterns are prevalent in our culture, and I can attest to their regular occurrence among the families in recovery.

Importantly, Satir tells us that these dysfunctional communication patterns are actually ways that members of a family try to *gain power and control over others* through covert ways. Let's examine these four dysfunctional styles along with the covert bid for power associated with each style:

Placating: A placating style is an attempt to get on someone's good side through people-pleasing gestures. The placater has no problem being the first to absorb blame and admit, "It's *my* fault." Missing in this response is genuine consideration and respect for the other person's selfhood. Placaters try to assume power and control in the relationship by leading others to feel guilty or to take pity on them. Unfortunately, a child begins to feel contempt for the parent who uses this style. Placating is a common feature of co-dependent relating.

Blaming: The blaming style takes an offensive position and is quick to point out weaknesses and limitations of others. The blamer says, "It's all *your* fault!" The blaming style assumes power in the relationship by leading others to feel powerless and fearful. A child who is blamed is usually so overwhelmed by guilt that she is unable to absorb any important information that may be transmitted. Eventually the child comes to feel resentment toward the blaming parent. Although she may not disclose these resentful feelings, she carries them with her for years.

Super Reasonable: This style of communication uses a lot of words to overwhelm the listener with the logic, superiority, and truth of the message. Power is gained as the child is made to feel stupid and inferior. This is the "mommy knows best" approach, which tries to convince the child that there is only one right way or answer and it belongs to the parent.

Irrelevance: This style catches the listener off guard by introducing information that does not pertain to the topic. Children can be masters at this form of communication as they distract and disrupt their parents. But parents, too, are capable of using an irrelevant style as a way of communicating to their children. For example: Johnny says, "Mom, when can I have my allowance?" Mom replies, "Johnny, I think your dad is calling from the back yard." The covert bid for power and control in this style of communication is gained when the other person (Johnny) is thrown off guard or loses balance.

As you become more aware of these dysfunctional communication styles in your family, notice the bids for power that are being sought. Try to place these four communication senders on the control continuum. (In actuality, they each would be at the far left of the continuum. Can you see why?)

Use family meetings to demonstrate more effective and honest styles of communicating with your children. Your first few attempts may not seem promising; you may become frustrated, but you can build on each new interaction.

Understanding

To make sure that your ideas are grasped by your child, you'll need to be fully immersed in the communication. One of the common, faulty patterns that I see with families in recovery is that parents talk to children distractedly. A mother may give orders to a young child while she is in the midst of hurriedly dressing for work: "And when you get home, remember to feed the dog, empty the trash, and unload the dishwasher. OK?"

The child, engrossed in a last-minute television show before going off in the morning car pool, answers a token "OK" but lets the words slip through one ear and out the other. When the frazzled Mom arrives home from work at the end of a long day, glancing at her watch to make sure she's going to make her twelve-step meeting on time, her child is back in front of the television, the dog is barking wildly for his evening meal, and the dishwasher is still packed from the night before.

A misunderstanding? Not really. The recovering mother is suffering from the single-parent syndrome where she tries to do too many things at the same time. Her communication was faulty. She used too many words, she allowed too little time for communicating, and she imparted too much information at once.

Remember that your child may have become skilled at not listening to you. Just as you have become a distracted speaker to the child whom you scarcely know anymore, so he has become a distracted listener. These dysfunctional patterns become ingrained and interfere with your ability to understand each other.

Ideally, the mother in the above scenario needs to use the *Stop, Look, and Listen!* technique when communicating her instructions to her child. Morning is probably *not* the best time of day to do this. She needs to shift to a time when they are each relaxed, perhaps the night before or the weekend. When communicating expectations, she needs to *Stop* any activity she's doing, sit down with her child face to face; to *Look* and make eye-contact; and to *Listen* as the child repeats back his understanding of her expectations. She may even want to discuss consequences and implement a behavioral chart to assist the child in his understanding.

When you communicate to a child—even to teens—you must keep your ideas simple and nonthreatening. Use fewer words and take the time that's needed to review expectations. Also, don't become frustrated if a child falls back into old behavior patterns. Try to make your child feel at ease by using a pleasant tone of voice, by smiling, and by providing a relaxed environment. Remember, too, that your child may have become hyperreactive to stress as a result of your chemical dependence. So, you'll want to offer soothing and reassurance even when discussing problem behaviors.

The following suggestion may provide help on how to keep your communications simple and nonthreatening: Offer a cup of herbal tea with honey and perhaps some graham crackers or other non-sugary snack food. (Children love this ritual of having tea up to the age of the teen years.) You, too, will feel more relaxed in the low-threat situation. Review the problem behaviors but add plenty of positive assertions. I even recommend starting with positive assertions, such as:

> Tim, you've been doing a great job of feeding the dog all week. I'm proud of you, and I know Fido is happier. I don't hear him barking when I come home from work. Sometimes, you've done pretty well with emptying the trash—at least three days out of five. That's a big improvement. But, what can *we* do to help you remember to empty the dishwasher? I don't think you've remembered to do that once this week. What would you suggest?

When she provides this open, low-threat forum, Tim's mother may be surprised at the information that her son will communicate to her about the dishwasher.

> I just hate doing that dumb old dishwasher. It never got to be my job until Dad left. I mean, *you* always used to do it. I feel like a sissy. And besides, I'm always afraid I might break some of the dishes, and then you'll get *really* mad. What if all of a sudden you start throwing dishes at me like you did *that one time*?

Tim has just revealed his real, inner experience. He *needs* to feel like a *boy*. The dishwasher is also a stress trigger because it symbolizes a time when his mother was drinking and her out-of-control behavior shocked and frightened him.

Tim's mother may not even remember some of the harsh verbal tirades that have fallen on her son's ears. But that child remembers. Some of her behavioral reactions were extreme, although she doesn't even recall the episode of throwing dishes when she was under the influence of alcohol. But Tim remembers.

By providing the low-threat communication forum, Tim's mother can negotiate a different chore. She might say:

> Thanks for explaining that to me, son. I see why you have a hard time with the dishwasher. I'd forgotten that time when I threw dishes at you—back when I was drinking. That is not something I ever want to do again. I'm sorry I frightened you. Will you forgive me? (pause) Now that I understand, let's come up with a different kind of chore. How about mowing the lawn instead? Thanks for opening up and talking to me about this.

Most of us prefer a calm, information-sharing meeting when we're in conflict with another adult (an employer, a spouse). Your children have this same need.

Information

Information about the world in which we live seems to be an area of lack in many children from chemically dependent families. Research with school-aged children from these homes has taught me a lot about their deficits in verbal information skills. Even children with good overall verbal abilities tend to show limitations in this one area of functioning. I have related this finding to similar observations that were made about adult children of alcoholics (ACoAs) by Kritsberg.[13]

> ACoAs as a rule do not possess *concrete information* on how to live life. When they were growing up, there was no one to answer their questions. When an ACoA says, "I don't know," or "I don't understand," it is not a lie. The lack of information is both in concrete knowledge and in the ability to deal with emotional states. (Italics mine.)

For this reason, I emphasize the parent's need to *teach*, to bring enrichment to children through regular interactions. Build discussions into family life on a regular basis. Talk to your child. Use words to communicate not only ideas but feelings. You can easily retranslate the information that you believe is too complicated for a child's mind into concepts simple enough for even very young children. The only material to be avoided is that which can overwhelm a child emotionally, such as information about specifics of your marital problems, financial problems, and employment problems.

To improve upon the exchange of information within the family, all family members need to practice. Your child will need to develop an improved ability to attend to what you're saying, to listen. You may have to identify your own faulty communication patterns that interfere with your ability to share information effectively.

Communicating by Words or Signals

In this period of recovery, your children are most likely to send "signals" about their inner hurt. Wordless signals. It is up to us to tune in to the child's inner world with empathy, to supply the missing words, to interpret the hidden feelings, and to translate the nonverbal messages. This is what is known as empathic attunement. We can come to understand and even experience our child's troubling and confusing inner states. Let me give an example.

Sometimes when I talk to a child about troubling information, that child will suddenly shift and ask for a glass of water. Interpretation? Often the child is telling me—without words—that the topic under discussion has become too disturbing. She is beginning to relive some of the stress and fears of the past. The disturbing discussion has aroused the child's nervous system. When she becomes afraid, her throat gets dry. As I attune myself to the child's inner world, I'm able to glimpse the terror that says "Stop! I'm feeling overwhelmed. Can we change the subject?" But the child's words merely say "Can I have a glass of water?"

At such times I respond to the child by helping her to articulate the inner experience. "It seems you're feeling scared all over again as we talk about your parents' fight when they were drinking. Maybe you'd rather play for a while now." (Introducing a self-soothing activity helps calm the child's fears.)

The child then comes to integrate this part of her self-experience in a new and important way. But most of all, she feels that I really do understand her and respect her needs.

Self-Monitoring

In the earliest days of your recovery, you learned to tune in to your inner world; you learned to listen, perhaps for the first time ever, to important cues about your own inner processes; you learned to identify whether you were too hungry, too angry, too lonely, or too tired; and you learned what you needed to do to take care of yourself properly.

Children from chemically dependent, co-dependent families are estranged from their inner processes. If indeed they were ever tuned in sensitively, they seem to have lost contact with their most basic ability to self-monitor. A parent's empathic responses during recovery can help children develop sensitivity and awareness. You can *teach* and guide your children towards an improved self-monitoring ability. *Teach* your children to identify angry feelings and to *own them* rather than to feel ashamed of them. *Teach* them to talk openly and honestly without fear of punishment. *Teach* children that they can admit loneliness rather than seek arousal. *Teach* your children that they can safely admit to being human, to being tired and needing to rest, or to being in need of your support. As children gain greater ability to self-monitor, they begin to develop a sense of confidence and self-mastery.

Joining

Gerald Jampolsky, a psychiatrist who teaches "attitudinal healing" in his work with terminally-ill children, tells us that all healing is self-healing.[14] The healing work that you are doing with your children will ultimately lead you further down the path of your own recovery. The common source for communicating with your child is the gateway of recovery that you have already entered. You know how it feels to be helpless, bewildered, and lonely. Now, through empathy, you can understand more when your child feels the same way. You join your child through your common need to rebuild a new, loving relationship.

Teach[8]

To give instruction to, to train.

To give to another knowledge or skill which one has oneself.

Throughout this chapter I have emphasized your role as *teacher*. You are the role model from whom your children will derive important, new learning. You also will actively *teach* some new, important lessons that you are just starting to learn yourself.

One of the keys to success for this stage of parent-child healing is parent *involvement*. You have been given a gift, a special privilege of being teacher and guide to your children, while helping make the world a better place through them. While you may be only a step or two ahead of them in terms of your own learning, you still have valuable information to impart. You, *the parent*, are the most important person to teach these new skills and attitudes to your children.

One of the most positive lights that I can shed on your recovery from chemical dependence is the following:

You have been given the opportunity to learn how to be
more humane to your children
than your parents were to you.
Through healing the hurt of your child,
through rebuilding that relationship,
you will teach.
And
the lessons which you teach,
will be carried forward
to the next generation
of tomorrow's
children.

11 | Healing the Hurt—ACT III

"After all these years, I've finally told my oldest that I really love him," Chuck shared, his eyes moist. "We've been going through family counseling with Buddy at his residential treatment center. The other night the words just popped outa my mouth."

"Well you're right on schedule," Karra said holding the outline for ACT III. "*Affection, consideration, and trust.* My three weakest suits. Guess the only way I've given *affection* is through gifts. Big, shiny, expensive ones. And *consideration* has been 'You scratch my back, I'll scratch yours.' But, *trust?* I don't know what that word even means."

"I used to think my girls trusted me," Mimi said sadly. "Now I'm not sure they even want to hear the word *love* from me anymore. I used to tell them all the time, back when Fred was drinking, 'Remember, Mommy loves you.' When he'd forget to come home for one of their birthdays or some special occasion, I'd say, 'Don't worry, Mommy loves you.'"

"Maybe they got burned out on love," Karra said.

"Nobody gets burned out on real love. It's a natural high, y'know?" Sara said.

"No, I don't know," Karra said.

"Your girls aren't so much burned out on your love, Mimi, but they could be tired of hearing the words. You and Chuck are opposites. He never said it, and you said it all the time. I think your girls want more *consideration* from you, now that they're older," Fred offered.

"Oh, I know. They want their 'space,'" Mimi said woefully.

"Fred's right. There's more than one way to express love to our kids. Like *acceptance,*" Chuck said. "Take the other night when my boy-twin walked into family counseling wearing this earring. I wanted to laugh out loud. Make a few jokes at his expense. I thought he looked like a kook. But for once I kept my big mouth shut."

"I noticed," Betsy said. "I was proud of you."

"Listen, man, you want a tip?" Sam said. "There's something more you could do for that boy-twin of yours to show consideration. Like, give him a *name*. The same goes for that adopted boy of yours. Didn't you name the poor kid yet, or what?"

"Yeah. Like, me and Sam been noticing some of you in here talk about your kids like they're not real," Sara explained. "Mimi and Fred do it all the time. 'Our youngest boy' this, and 'the girls' that. Like, you got anonymous human beings living at your house?"

"Hey, Sam and Sara, I wanna say this with a straight face," Chuck began. "But I bet you two could teach the rest of us in here a lot about *love*. I mean, the two of you living like such free spirits and all. So, I'm trying to keep an open mind, listen to what you say, and not get defensive. But for a minute there you caught me off guard. Now I know Sam wears his earring, too, but I never meant that *he* looked like a kook. Just for the record, my boy-twin does have a name, Charles Junior, named after me. Our oldest son, Buddy, got the name of Betsy's deceased father, him dying right before the boy was born. And then our youngest son came to us with his own name, Christopher. But I gotta say again, Sam, I got no problems with your earring—if it makes you happy."

"Who cares what you think of my earring, man? I'm just glad that your kids have names."

"Every kid deserves a name," Karra said. "And he deserves to hear it, too. I don't remember my mom every calling me by name. It was always 'Clumsy.' Or 'Stupid.' Sara's right. Mimi, you do talk about your daughters as though they're joined like Siamese triplets."

It's just a bad habit," Mimi said. "Now, take the students in my classroom. I'm so good at remembering each and every name, sometimes for several years afterwards."

"Now that we're learning about this Affection Phase," Karra said, "'I need to pass a little affection around to each of you. No big, shiny presents for everyone. Just a hugful of affection. I'm going to miss each of you when this series is over. So why do we have to end? This is one place where I've been able to talk about my problems with my kids and not feel like a fool. Or ashamed. Or bad."

"Hey, you pulled the words right outa my mouth," Chuck said. "Our family counseling meetings with Buddy have been a big help, but we're not open in the same way as we are in here. We can't admit that we don't know how to be parents."

"Or that sometimes we don't even want to be parents," Betsy said.

"I'm just starting to learn how to be a dad," Fred said. "And that's all thanks to this group."

"So why do we have to end?" Sara repeated Karra's question.

"Yeah. Like we could start another *series*. I bet there's still a lot of A-C-Ts in the dictionary for us chemically dependent parents. Like Acid, Coke, and Tranqs. Sorry, guys! That was a bad joke."

"You're talking about a *new* series, and I still need to finish this one," Mimi said nervously. "I don't know as much about love as I thought I did. Let's start our class on ACT III and learn about this Affection Phase."

The Affection Phase

Three important attitudes—*affection, consideration,* and *trust*—are presented as the stabilizing features of the new family in recovery. This is

ACT III—the culmination of all your previous efforts to rebuild relationships with your children. Slowly, through the ACT I and ACT II processes, a new relationship has come about with each child. What you sense most about this relationship is that it has been built upon the principles of mutual respect. Your children have come to trust the positive changes of your recovery. You have learned to see each of them as separate, unique, and valuable.

Perhaps somewhere into the second year of your recovery, your family gradually moves into a period of harmony and closeness. Among the family members there is a sense of belonging to this new family in recovery. Parental leadership has been restored through your renewed commitment. Many of the ACT II conflicts and power struggles are being resolved. As a result of your renewed leadership, a feeling of safety has been guaranteed to your children. Natural family role positions are carried out more adaptively as we parents go about the business of being parents and kids get to be kids.

Family members are finally beginning to feel secure enough to risk being vulnerable and real with each other. As a result of working through the control struggles and resolving them, a new period of family intimacy begins. That is why I consider this period of family development as the Affection Phase. This is the time that you will want to concentrate on the three important attitudes of ACT III that are necessary for healing the hurt: *affection, consideration,* and *trust.*

AFFECTION[8]

Tender Attachment.

Love.

A settled goodwill.

Fondness, tender feelings.

All human beings have a need for affection. This is the last of the three basic human needs that psychologist W. C. Schutz emphasizes as essential to living a mentally healthy life. In addition to a need for belonging and the need for mastery and control in our lives, our most pressing need is to experience tender attachment within our own families. Children need to feel attached to parents, and spouses need to feel a sense of tender attachment to each other.

"Oh, no, how co-dependent!" You may be thinking as you scratch *tender attachment* from the top of the above list. You'll show affection through a settled goodwill, fondness and tender feelings, or love, most certainly. But attachment? No way!

The concept of co-dependence can become distorted and used as a defense by those of us who have problems with attachment. When we fear submitting to closeness, we can always pull back from others and use the buzz world of the hour, "Hey, this feels too much like co-dependence. It's unhealthy, you know?" When our childhood attachment to a parent-figure has resulted in being exploited in some way, we are likely to shun closeness. Many children from chemically dependent families have basic problems in achieving a sense of attachment and bondedness to parents.[1,6]

Problems in Attachment in Chemically Dependent Families

The "hurt that binds" is that type of closeness or enmeshment that does not affirm selfhood. When we use other people—including our children—to make us feel whole or complete, we begin to experience them as a psychological part of us. We don't see them as separate or unique, and we have difficulty recognizing their needs because we're so focused on our own person or our own needs. We may not even be aware that this leaves the other person feeling devalued. When we value others solely for the functions that they provide and the roles that they fulfill for us, we have trouble seeing them as real. As separate and distinct from us. When they let us know that they have their own point of view, we can become quite angry. Behind the anger is fear. It's almost as if they were abandoning us physically!

We may have grown up with the illusion of closeness, where we were used by our parents. This may have seemed like bonding or tender attachment. But we are left with a profound sense of emptiness—a deep, intrapersonal isolation—that is so much a part of life in chemically dependent families. How can we experience suffocating closeness and feel alienated at the same time?

Some years ago I was conducting my first research with children of recovering alcoholic parents, and I began to wonder about their attachment to their parents.[6] I was surprised by the research results that revealed that these youngsters did *not* experience attachment to their parents. Despite what they may have described superficially as closeness to one or both parents, their inner psychological picture was one of alienation. The child may have lived in an everyday world of parents and siblings, but his inner world revealed that he was a social isolate. What does this mean?

Over the years I have continued to hear of this sense of "isolation" explained by adults in recovery. Even among a group of people, we may feel that we're on the outside, looking in. We know that this subjective state of isolation is a part of the dis-EASE of chemical dependence. (It begins as the NO ONE Syndrome for kids.) We know that we can gather together in large groups of people and still feel an inner sense of isolation and emptiness. This is what keeps us coming back to the bar, the tavern, the party, or wherever others gather together to drink and use. But these gatherings do not have the lasting ability to remove the inner isolation.

Regardless of whether we engage in people-pleasing and partying or whether we pull away from others completely, we try to assuage our hurt. We desperately long for human warmth and caring.

And so it is with our children.

The Child's Need for Parental Support and Attachment

In Chapter 6, I described my research related to school-aged children of recovering alcoholics. These youngsters taught me three important notions: (1) They were not attached to their parents; (2) They had lacked parental support and guidance during highly stressful times in their lives—even after the parent had gained sobriety; and (3) They still desperately needed and wanted emotional support or tender attachment from their parents.

As you begin to rebuild relationships with your children, you can expect their ambivalence. They feel two ways about you at the same time. They need your support but fear that you *cannot* or *will not* give it.

When you and your children were resolving your differences during ACT II, you and they began to experience the closeness of joining. Your children were reassured by this, even though they resisted it. Their resistance was to closeness. A child who has had to rely on himself fears admitting that he is wrong. During ACT III, children come to learn that they will not lose selfhood by accepting your support and caring.

Resistance to Closeness

What are some of the ways that you have kept from being close to your children? Your spouse? Your friends? You can expect three characteristic behaviors as you attempt family closeness. These are some of the old behaviors that may have been present in you as well as in your family before you began recovery. Rejection, avoidance, and antagonism are the defenses that crop up again.

Rejection

Rejecting behaviors are expressed in a variety of subtle and not-so-subtle ways. When a child is speaking to us about something of interest or importance to him, we may turn away to some activity of our own, walk into another room, or tell the child "Keep quiet! I'm trying to listen to the news." We may reject a child's attempts at closeness through our distracted behaviors, such as cleaning, cooking, or washing the family car instead of spending time with the youngster. We may reject one child in favor of another in the family, such as Karra's rejection of Billy for Sandy. The closeness that Billy sought from his mother led Karra to push him away. Billy's clinging was uncomfortable for Karra.

At times a spouse may reject his marital partner for one of the children. (Betsy appeared to bring the adopted boy into the family to help fill the emotional needs that were missing in her relationship with Chuck.) Or one spouse may reject another because of the fear of intimacy. To fill in the gaps missing in the relationship, he or she may use relationships outside the family, such as extended family members, sponsors, friends, and even counselors.

Avoidance

When a spouse, parent, or child resists family closeness, that individual may decide to use avoidance behaviors. We can avoid an intimate family gathering by "forgetting" that an important family meal was scheduled. Or we may arrive late enough so that we don't have to engage in too much togetherness. Or a child may suddenly show up with a couple of friends announcing that they would like to join us. The intimate family occasion then becomes a more casual and less threatening occasion for that child—and for others in the family, as well.

Workaholic behaviors on the part of adults can sometimes be ways to avoid closeness. A real workaholic may deny the implications of what I'm saying and insist, "No way am I afraid of closeness! I'm *choosing* to work long hours to get that promotion with the pay raise that everyone in the family wants and needs." However, the person on the receiving end of workaholic avoidance, such as a spouse who's kept waiting or a child who is left for long periods at childcare, knows about the distancing aspects of workaholism.

You can even express avoidance to family closeness and intimacy through some of the important and necessary aspects of recovery. Taking on too many obligations in the self-help community, for example, may result in the same kind of energy drain as workaholism.

When you come home at the end of a long day after having spent your energies in career, altruistic, or recovery activities, you have little enthusiasm left over to give to your children. You may dole out no more than a bedtime kiss or a few minutes of casual conversation. That is your token gesture, and it seems to be enough. But is it *enough* for your children?

Antagonism

Antagonism is something that crops up unexpectedly when we begin to criticize and find fault in our children. Suddenly, after days and perhaps even weeks of asserting, teaching, and communicating effectively, you begin to feel an attack of the "negatives" coming on. You don't like anything about the way your child is behaving. Let's consider Karra and Angel as a case in point. Karra knew how to rely on Angel when the child acted as a family caretaker, but in recovery she didn't know how to reach out to Angel as a separate and distinct individual. She didn't know how to show affection or consideration. Small wonder! Karra had never experienced tender affection during her own childhood. She simply didn't know how to acknowledge Angel in a non-critical way.

Sometimes children also use antagonism as a resistance to closeness. You've just planned the first birthday party for your child since you began your recovery. You went to a lot of trouble to make that child see how much you care. Then, all during the party, your ungrateful ten-year-old acts antagonistic and reverts to old, troubled behavior patterns, seemingly unaware of your hurt feelings. At times like this, watch your reactions! You may find yourself in a victim role. How easily the rejection feeling brings up your own antagonism. You start to think about how selfish this kid really is!

At such frustrating times, try not to focus on the disturbing or disappointing interaction. Instead, try to be aware of your child's troubled inner state. How confused she must be! Her behavior is communicating a deep sense of fear and mistrust that screams, "I'm afraid to let you be nice to me!" The child's fear stems from her wobbly sense of self. She still doesn't know how to handle a situation in which she experiences so much positive attention. Your former criticisms may still echo in her ear; she is certain that she is bad and undeserving. She needs your reassurance—with words—that you love her, no matter what.

Love

Perfect love casts out fear.[15]

Fear prevents the expression of love. Sometimes, the more obvious block may seem to be a wall of anger and hostility, but behind that wall of anger is invariably an even greater wall of fear.

During ACT II the basic fear was of expressing the hostility that came from realizing differences and trying to resolve them. *The one fear more potent than expressing hostility is the fear of giving and receiving love.*

What is this *perfect* love that can overcome fear or that can help us overcome the usual hurdles and resistances to forming loving relationships with our children? Psychologists who have written along these lines might refer to "perfect love" as unconditional love. Twelve-step programs also stress the notion of complete acceptance and unconditional love:

> And acceptance is the answer to *all* my problems today. When I am disturbed, it is because I find some person, place, thing, or situation—some fact of my life—unacceptable to me, and I can find no serenity until I accept that person, place or thing or situation as being exactly the way it is supposed to be at this moment.[10]

Love is the balm of all healing. But the giving and receiving of perfect love—the love that casts out fear—is preceded by complete acceptance.

Accepting each of your children exactly as they are at any moment in time is crucial for healing the hurt. This will be far more healing than all the birthday parties that you plan, all the gifts that you buy, or all the opportunities for lessons and activities that you may want to provide. Somewhere deep inside, a child who experiences total acceptance from a parent or any adult feels loved. This little child's eyes are a little brighter, her smile more radiant, and her expression more trusting when she sees us.

A child who experiences a lack of acceptance also knows it. This child will seem more wary and guarded as he anticipates the next criticism or the next reminder that maybe he should do something this way or that way or some way other than the way that he would like to do it. In order to win acceptance and approval, he must continue to strive to do better or differently—the way that you would have him do it.

A child who does not experience total acceptance is grumpy and antagonistic as he continues to defend against a parent's subtle rejection. You can reflect on your own experience in recovery to appreciate how this child feels. Sometime during your recovery, you must have tried to do your best, only to have someone suggest that you were still a little off target or not quite up to *their* standards. Recall your first reaction. A Wall of Fear, perhaps followed by anger. The expression of perfect love does not *instill* fear; it *dissolves* it!

A Settled Goodwill

When your family's resistances to affection throw you off balance, you may be tempted to return to the previous stage—ACT II; you may want to reassert yourself, to communicate a little more fervently, or to teach and lecture a little more intensely than before. Resist those temptations.

Instead, return to the primary activities of ACT I. Increase your awareness of your family's resistances. Try to look at the problem from their perspectives. Renew your *commitment* to your children by using the same methods that you used in ACT I. And, be generous with the *time* that your family needs to ease more gently into the Affection Phase. Try to steer clear of the negative feeling states that are a part of the ACT II processes. In other words, don't try to *assert*, *control*, or *teach* at this point. *Go back to the basics* of team building. If you don't do this, you may wind up without a team! A family can stay stuck in the control phase processes forever. This often happens in recovery, where life is spent trying to win power struggles. The processes of ACT II, or the control phase, are *safe*. When we're locked into a power struggle, we don't ever have to advance towards closeness and intimacy.

Amends

An amends is most simply, "I'm sorry." To make amends is to admit to others that we are *aware that we have hurt them*. Too often we don't like to make amends because we think this action is the admission that we have lost a battle or that we have given up a part of our self to the other. But making amends has to do with forgiveness, both asking for it and making possible another's giving it and receiving it. We all think that forgiveness is a fine and necessary part of healing. But how often do we recognize that we need to help another person *release* resentments? How often do we say "Will you forgive me?"

Perhaps you've already gone through an amends-making process with your children, but just because you've said "Sorry" once doesn't mean that you can't and shouldn't say the healing word again. Incorporate the amends-forgiveness process as an ongoing part of your family relationships. You will continue to make mistakes with your children; you'll want to acknowledge those mistakes promptly. This doesn't mean that you have to go around on your knees every day. But it does mean that you are willing to admit your recognition of your mistakes to your children and that you are willing to help free them of the hurt they may carry.

Expanding awareness helps you recognize new sources of fear and confusion that may still be present in your children. Any time that you become aware of areas of hurt that you have contributed, you need to face your child honestly with the conviction of your new value system.

A part of the moral inventory of the fourth step of Alcoholics Anonymous emphasizes the word *moral* as opposed to *immoral*. A part of the goal for the new family in recovery is a new set of standards or values by which to live. As recovering parents, we have the principles of the twelve steps to guide us. But our children will continue to look to us as models for standards to emulate or defy. When we base our standards on sound, wholesome principles of living, our children will more readily accept our values. But we must recognize that our children are also going to be watching for our inconsistencies. Double standards will undermine our efforts. So we must practice what we preach and walk like we talk.

As we attempt to establish ourselves as loving, forgiving, and honest human beings, no process is more important than the amends-forgiveness process.

If love is the balm of healing, forgiveness is the container for that balm. Children are very forgiving. Unlike adults, children can use our sincere apology to almost completely erase their painful memories. They are not, by nature, grievance collectors. The key for your youngster is this: make your amends *specific*; accept complete responsibility for the act that you did that harmed your child; and verbalize back to the child that you know that you hurt her by these actions:

> I'm sorry that I burdened you many times, Susie, when I left you alone at night with your baby sister. You were too young for those responsibilities, and you must have been very frightened and angry with me. I was wrong to leave you alone when I went out partying. I want you to know that I will not hurt you in this same way again. Will you forgive me?

Many of us ponder the question, "But I did so many wrongs to my child. Am I supposed to go about saying 'Sorry' for each and every one?" Not necessarily. But as you deepen your awareness of your child, you will come to recognize those hurts that were most traumatic. Your child needs you to reflect back to her your awareness of her inner state.

Avoid the ever-so-brief amends that say simply "Sorry, Susie, for anything I did to hurt you when I was drinking and using." This blank-check amend leaves the child with the responsibility of filling in the blank—one more time—as she goes about picking up the pieces for you. Nor should you try to explain away your behavior through excuses or rationalizations: "Well, of course, the reason I was grumpy with you, Susie, was because of your *father's* drinking problem. . . ."

The forgiveness coin has two sides: We seek forgiveness, and we extend it to others. Psychiatrist Gerald Jampolsky said,

> Forgiveness is possibly the concept most central to attitudinal healing and yet it is also the one most likely to be misunderstood. Most people understand that deep urges for goodness exist in everyone's heart no matter how overlayered they may be with guilt, defensiveness, dishonesty and inhumanity. Forgiveness looks past the more superficial motivations of the individual, no matter how extreme these may be, to the place in his heart where he yearns for exactly what we yearn for. Everyone wants peace and safety. Everyone wants to make a difference. And everyone wants to release his potential for love. It is deep into this desire that forgiveness gazes. And seeing there a reflection of itself, it releases the other from judgment.[14]

CONSIDERATION[8]

Careful not to hurt the feelings of others or cause inconvenience to them.

Attentive respect.

Appreciative regard.

Now that you have acknowledged the hurt that you may have contributed in the past, the first act of *consideration* for your children is to spare them additional hurt. Of course, you may sometimes inconvenience your children or hurt their feelings. But you will continue to acknowledge these errors as they occur. Thus, you will keep your new relationship free of resentment and hostility. Because you are human, you will not carry out parenting perfectly—not ever—even with the fullest dedication. But the important neutralizer for hurt is your prompt admission that you were wrong. An ego-attack may still lead you to want to blame others. You want to be right no matter what. Hopefully you will come to realize that one of the keys to rebuilding a relationship with your children—or with anyone—is overcoming the ego.

Attentive Respect

Do you look down on your children or do you greet them as wonderful beings, deserving of your respect?

Attentive respect is one of the most important attitudes that we can provide to a child. This is the attitude most necessary for empathic attunement or for tuning in to the inner world of the child. Attentive respect means that you listen to your child's ideas rather than to your own; you see your child's needs as legitimate and distinct from your own; you recognize your child's individuality as a blessing rather than a hindrance or curse.

This leads me to share with you a poem by Kahlil Gibran that I often share with other parents when I emphasize respect for a child.

Children

... Your children are not your children

They are the sons and daughters of

Life's longing for itself.

They come through you

But not from you.

Though they are with you,

Yet they belong not to you.

You may give them your love,

But not your thoughts . . .

For their souls dwell in the house

Of tomorrow which you cannot visit,

Not even in your dreams.

You may strive to be like them,

But seek not to make them like you . . .

For life goes forward and tarries

Not with yesterday.[16]

When a child is treated as a person worthy of respect, he will amaze you with his ability to respond back with respectful behavior.

Appreciative Regard

How do you express appreciation to your child just for who he is? Do you let him know that you are grateful that he has come into your life? Do you tell him through words or actions?

A child needs to *hear* you express appreciative regard. His most pressing need is to feel valued, respected, and appreciated just for *who* he is, not for what he *does*, and not for keeping his chores or homework current. He wants your appreciation for the unique human being—the one rosebud unlike any other in the garden—that he is.

A child needs to see the gleam in your eyes when you greet him; he needs to see your joyful face as you interact with him. He needs to feel the warmth of your embrace in a hug of gratitude that expresses appreciation through contact.

All these ways of expressing appreciation help neutralize the computer-like existence of our modern age where all family members spend too much time in the fast lane. Don't try to compensate on weekends, holidays, and summer vacations. Appreciative regard costs you nothing. You can lavish your child daily with something more lasting than Nintendo. Saying "I am so glad, my child, that you are YOU" takes few words and so little energy or time.

Some use alcohol, cigarettes or drugs

as a medicine for their mind

but as any medicine

too much is no good.

Neurotics depend on holidays, weekends,

and days-off.

Those who cultivate

their APPRECIATION
celebrate
DAILY.[17]

TRUST[8]

Confidence in a person because
of the qualities one perceives.

A responsibility involving
the confidence of others.

Faith in the future.

Why do we hear so little about trust in our wonderful, healing world of chemical dependence? In many ways our field has picked up the humanistic threads of how to treat others with more acceptance, tolerance, and compassion. And we also hear about love. Self-esteem. Choices. Intimacy. And now, healing. But what about *trust*?

Those of us who have grown up in chemically dependent or other types of dysfunctional families often don't know very much about trust. Like Karra, our childhood experiences provided us with every good reason to be *mistrustful*. Then what happens? Karra carries this same attitude into her relationship with her children, and before long they, too, learn that people—the ones closest to them—are not to be trusted. Unless healed, our children's attitudes of mistrust will be carried forward into the next generation.

Trust means that we have *confidence in a person because of the qualities we perceive in him*. When you were learning to look at your child with new awarenesses in recovery, what qualities did you see? As you came to appreciate and respect the talents and virtues of your child, didn't those qualities seem to become more vivid?

"What-you-see-is-who-I'll-be."

As *trust* guides your vision of your children, you begin to highlight their strengths and positive attributes.

By now you've begun to realize that your child has an *inner* self that is unique and special. This self wants to flourish and grow and heal. The more trust you place in your child's potential to emerge, the more opportunities you'll begin to create to make sure this happens. History tells us the stories of exceptional children, such as the Helen Kellers of the world who were thought to be hopelessly deaf, mute, or lost to mental autism and mental retardation. Then, along came a loving caregiver who saw beyond appearances and helped bring forth that child's special gifts and talents.

When your children experience you as supporting and trusting the best in them, they'll come to feel more trusting of you. If you concentrate on their deficiencies or their lack, you'll drive them back behind the false front of rigid defenses.

As with forgiveness, to extend trust is to receive it back in return. Mutual trust between you and your child begins when you stop seeing your child as a family role or a behavior problem or a threat to your serenity. *Try to focus on your child's strongest points and ignore what you believe to be his weaknesses.*

Think about your own process of recovery. When you stopped focusing on all your own blemishes and began to highlight and affirm your attributes, energy was released for developing your personal best.

You found out that you didn't need chemicals to exist. Abusive, destructive relationships didn't need to continue. You could move out into the clear light of day and really begin to live life.

If perfect love casts out fear, it also paves the way for a trusting relationship between you and your children.

Faith in the Future

Growing up in dysfunctional families, we learned basic attitudes of mistrust, pessimism, cynicism, and judgments. We must overcome these negative states of mind for they will sabotage us now, just as they have in the past, unless we begin to shift gears and develop a new way of seeing life and our relation to it.

A step beyond trust is faith. Faith is the positive application of the mind to some belief or hope. As parents in recovery, we hope that our children will be healed of their hurt. Now we come to *believe* that this will happen.

We'll need to use positive attitudes that can begin with the simple conviction, "I believe . . ."

"I *believe* that communication with my child is being improved."

"I *believe* that my child's hurt is being healed."

"I *believe* that I am a good and decent parent."

"I *believe* that my child is *trusting* my parenting."

"I *believe* that I am showing *consideration* to my child."

"I *believe* that I can be *affectionate* with my child."

"I *believe* that I am *teaching* my child a better way of life."

"I *believe* that I am *communicating* more clearly with my child."
(Or communicating more openly, more honestly, etc.)

"I *believe* that I am *asserting* myself in positive ways with my child."

"I *believe* that I am devoting quality *time* to my child."

"I *believe* that I am *committed* to healing the hurt of my child."

"I *believe* that I am *aware* of the unique self of my child."

Begin each affirmation in the present tense, as though it is happening at this very moment, now. Use the name of your child in each statement to personalize the effect. Create other positive affirmations. Write these on note cards and carry them in your pocket, or put them someplace where you are most likely to see them. The cards will serve as subliminal reminders. During the course of the day, rehearse your affirmations silently. Your positive beliefs as applications of faith will help you overcome some of your feelings of limitation and negativity. When you begin to doubt, you can simply use more positive affirmations to overcome your doubts. Apply these affirmations to the specific acts of healing, going all the way back to the beginning of the first ACT. This simple exercise offers surprising results.

Faith has long been associated with healing. Faith is *the* component of mystical healings, commonly referred to as "faith healings." You can apply this faith to "What-you-see-is-who-I'll-be," remembering to see the positive in your children. They'll experience themselves as people of worth.

And now in our ACTs of healing, we have come full circle back to *awareness*. Most journeys are fulfilled when we return home. That is where the journey of faith will lead us. In the practice of the Eastern philosophy of Zen, *faith* is actually derived from *awareness*, that sixth sense or intuitive way of knowing.

Faith is finally the end result of what some people call enlightenment or full spiritual awakening. One dedicated student of Zen finally reached enlightenment, and this is what he shared of that experience:

> Now for the first time I experience the joy that comes with an overpowering sense of *faith*. Before, my *faith* was limited to the rock-bottom minimum . . . I was embarrassed and uneasy when anyone spoke of *faith* . . . Now, with a great leap *faith* extended far and wide. It did not seem like *faith* at all but surest, clearest knowledge. The lines written by a Chinese mystic appeared in my head:

> *All shall be well*
> *and all shall be well*
> *and all manner of things*
> *shall be well.*[18]

Proceed with faith—with full awareness—of the precious gift to life that is your child and *all shall be well*.

12 | Finale

"We've made a decision. All of us together, as a team," Karra said. "We know that this was supposed to be our last discussion meeting to talk about what we've learned and to review resources for outside help, but we don't want *this* group to end."

"We still need help in parenting, and some of our children still need professional help," Mimi said.

"What we've learned is that we still need to keep learning," Fred said.

"Like, a little bit of knowledge can be dangerous," Sam said.

"Hey, we're just starting to see some changes in our kids," Chuck said. "Me, I've got some kids that still need professional help, like Buddy who's in residential treatment He's also got a court hearing coming up about abusing that girl. And Charles and Cassandra—that's my boy-twin and Sassy—well, they're still in their outpatient group. But Bitsy and me need help to be parents together."

"We want to contract for more meetings," Mimi said.

"But if we can't keep going with you as leader, we're ready to strike out on our own. I mean, we'll strike out together as a group," Karra volunteered.

Sara, who had been quiet up to now, began to talk through tears that were streaming down her face. "It's not just any group. It's *this* group with these people that I've come to love. We've gone through a lot together, and I trust these people as my friends. I respect them, too. I know they're trying to make a better way of life for their children. That gives me hope to do the same."

"Hey, Sara, you've lost your street talk! You sounded kinda like a *real* grown-up lady when you spoke just now," Chuck said.

"It'd blow your mind if you knew about my life before the streets," Sara said laughing. "But I guess that old upper crust training is still there deep inside me. Neither Sam nor I came from chemically dependent families."

"*Who* are you guys? Narcs under cover?" Chuck asked.

"No, my father was a preacher. A *pastor* and dean of a seminary. All my life I had to live by these strict, phony rules that were choking the life out of me. When I was about twelve, I smoked a little weed, and *Hallelujah!* I knew I'd found salvation.

"By the time I was sixteen, I was in the streets. That's where I met Sam. He saw me as a free-spirited creature, and I saw him as knowing his way around the drug world. We just hooked up together, and I guess you could say we've been hooked on each other ever since. Don't *even* ask Sam about his before-and-after life."

"C'mon, Sam, it's time to level with us, or we might decide to vote you out of our free-spirited group," Karra chided.

"My dad was a sawbones," Sam said. "Surgeon. Like a brain surgeon, y'know? Don't look at me that way, group. I'm not tripping. I'll give you his name and you can look him up in the phone book, give him a call, and ask him about his oldest son, Samuel Junior. He'll probably hang up on you because I'm the disappointment of his life. I'm the one that was supposed to be a FAX copy of him. All my brothers and sisters are yuppies, but Yo! I had to be ME."

"The family's never seen Seth—their only grandson," Sara said. "I hope they'll want to after we get our lives together a bit more. I hurt that Sam can't have family, and I hurt for me, too; but I hurt most for Seth. He's lost out on an extended family."

"That's why you folks are so important to us," Sam said. "You've become our family. Guess we didn't realize how bad we needed you until we started thinking that the group was going to end."

"So what about it?" Fred said, turning to me. "Are you willing to put up with us for another series?"

"I'm more than willing, because you are a very dedicated group. It would be so easy for me to say 'yes.' But I sincerely believe that you're able to carry on together, helping each other without any sort of leader."

"You mean like my AA meetings?" Chuck asked.

"Yes, a self-help group of sorts. But with a focus on helping each other heal the hurt of your children."

"If we don't do it, no one will," Karra said.

"The old NO ONE Syndrome again," Chuck said. "So, how do we get started? Do we need some kind of rule book?"

"I think you only need each other, your willingness, and the same twelve steps that the other Anonymous programs use."

"Then how's this any different from Parents Anonymous?" Mimi asked.

"Well, I'd say your starting point, your commonality, is your own recovery from chemical dependence. Then, you're talking specifically about the ways that being a chemically dependent parent has brought hurt to your children. The important idea is that you're interested in seeing your children as joining you in a parallel course of recovery. You recognize that their need to recover is based on a lot of unspoken hurts that may show up as actual problems now or later."

"And that's it in a nutshell?" Fred asked.

"In a nutshell," I said.

"Sounds simple, group, so how about it?" Karra said.

Hands raised unanimously to Karra's request.

"But I'm just a little nervous," Mimi added. "Suppose we get in trouble? What if our children develop problems that we can't handle?"

"The group shouldn't *replace* other resources in the community who are able to provide you with help," I explained. "What you're continuing to do is to keep each other *aware*, free from denial, about the hurt that you've contributed to your children and how to heal that hurt. The importance of the support group is to recognize that none of you has to be alone in your parenting. None of you has to suffer in secret or silence about the ongoing problems that you're having with your children. Research tells us that parents can drastically reduce their harmful actions towards their children when they have a recovering, supportive network."

"That eases my mind," Chuck said. "I don't want to bring harm to any of my kids anymore, not even to little Christopher."

"Will you help us write out the steps or retranslate them for our group?" Mimi asked.

"Of course."

"And what if we should get into trouble? I mean, look at the problems Chuck's had with his kids," Sara said. "We need to know how to get help and where."

"That's so important," Mimi said. "After my experience with the doctor and the buzzing blanket, I want to make sure that we all know how to make better choices for professional help."

"Everybody seems to have forgotten but me," Karra said proudly. "I remember that part of our wrap-up for tonight had to do with a discussion of *outside resources*. Are we ready to begin to talk about those?"

When to Seek Professional Assistance for Your Child

Chemical Use and Destructive Acts

Certain problems may affect the lives of our children in such a way that they require professional help. Destructive acts to self, others, or property by your child mean that he is crying out for more help than you can provide. Consult a mental health professional to guide you in how to provide help. As we've just seen, Chuck acted as a responsible and loving parent when he intervened in the lives of his three older children by getting them into treatment. Any time a child or adolescent is using or abusing alcohol or other drugs, it's best to consult a chemical dependence specialist at once.

When your children show problems of a critical nature, beware of your tendency to rationalize away your concerns. "I'm not *sure* if he's really on drugs. What if I'm wrong? Maybe I'll hurt him even worse if I take him for help." If you are wrong, the child will not be hurt through your intervention. If you have reason to believe that your child is dependent on alcohol or other drugs, you must act on your hunches and seek out an intervention specialist. These two critical areas—chemical dependence and destructive behaviors—are complicated in children and adolescents by their immaturity, peer group influence, and developmental problems, such as learning disabilities or attention deficit disorders (ADD).

Rely on your Parents in Recovery self-help support to assist you in strengthening your parenting support to the child who is severely troubled, but seek help for your child from an appropriate profes-sional.

Problems That Indicate Your Child Needs Help

Attention and Concentration
Short attention span.
Easily distractible.
Can't concentrate.

Destructive with Self and Others
Aggressive. Steals. Lies.
Sets fires. Self-abusive.
Harms others or belongings of others.

Emotional Problems
Temper outbursts. Tantrums.
Emotional ups and downs.
Depression. Moodiness. Irritability.
Cries often.

Interpersonal Problems
Problems with siblings and peers—
argumentative, resentful, jealous, faultfinding, angry.
Feels disliked by others.

Nutritional Problems
Binges on junk food and sugars. Hoards
or steals food. Obese. Doesn't eat regularly.
Anorexic. Underweight.

Obsessive-Compulsive Symptoms
Perfectionistic. Rigid. Driven. Has rituals,
such as needing to do things a certain way.

Physical Complaints
Stomachache. Headache. Nausea.
Vomiting. Tiredness. Frequent vague
pains such as "growing pains." Joint pains, etc.

School Problems
Behavior or academic problems.
Learning problems. Speech problems.
Truancy. Doesn't like school.
Complains about teachers. Driven.
Compulsive. Striving.

Self-Esteem Problems
Feels ugly, fat, or otherwise
unacceptable. Overly concerned with
appearance and with being liked or
popular. Grandiose. Inflated sense of
self-importance.

Self-Regulation Problems
Anxious. Hyper. Unsettled. Restless.
Becomes disorganized under stress.
Problems in elimination, such as
bedwetting, soiling, delayed toilet
training.

Sleep Disturbances
Nightmares. Insomnia. Sleepwalking.
Frequent bad dreams. Afraid to
sleep alone.

The above list identifies some of the problems commonly seen in children from chemically dependent families. We may think of these problems as occurring on a continuum from severe to mild. Depending on the severity of the problem (how often, how much), you also may need to consult a professional such as a family physician or your children's pediatrician for some of your concerns. Nutritional problems, physical complaints, self-regulation problems, and sleep disturbances are examples of the kind of problems that may require medical intervention.

Where to Find Professional Help
How do you find a mental health professional who specializes in work with children from chemically dependent families? Often a referral can be obtained by contacting treatment or recovery facilities. You can also use the yellow pages of your phone book to obtain referral services for psychologists, social workers, and family counselors who specialize in work with children and adolescents.

I recommend an initial consultation or face-to-face interview with the professional before you begin to contract for services. Often the specialist will charge nothing for this initial consultation. During this interview you discover if you can trust the professional. You want to determine if he or she embraces the principles of treatment that are compatible with those of your recovering community. To do this, ask potential helpers about their experience in using self-help support groups, such as twelve step programs; about their view of family recovery; and about their understanding of family reorganization and rebuilding relationships with children. Don't be reluctant to interview the professional and ask any questions you deem important to lead you to more informed decision making. Most important of all, discover if your child feels at ease with this helper who is to become an intimate part of his child's life.

You'll also want to know about the professional's experience in working with children from chemically dependent families, especially younger children. Ask if the professional is able to provide you with a complete assessment or psychological evaluation of your children's problems. This assessment is one that takes into consideration the child's level of maturity, both emotionally and intellectually. It is very important that the professional provide you with feedback about the results of your child's assessment and work collaboratively with you to help you help your child. If the professional cannot perform the evaluation, ask about a consultation with a professional who can provide the assessment.

How Long Will Your Child Require Outside Assistance?

When your child becomes involved in a professional helping relationship, either for chemical dependence or other problems, you may question "How long is this going to take?"

Remember my earlier caution against expecting quick and easy solutions. A certain behavior problem, such as a parent-child problem, may be readily accessible to intervention. Change can happen within a few weeks. But other problems will be very resilient and may take a much longer period of time to resolve. Don't feel that you are the worse parents for it if your child requires ongoing counseling for a period of time. Healing is not always immediate. Some might argue that behavior problems can be "cured" rather quickly; but when we talk about healing the *hurt* and the family processes of recovery, we're not dealing with a discrete behavior. We're dealing with complex family relationships.

Also, your child may need periods of assistance at various different points in his growing up experience. Certain expectable developmental positions are especially turbulent for children from chemically dependent families. Thirteen is one such age. Adolescence in general is a period of upheaval subject to the whimsy of peer group influences.

Your child and you may need to move in and out of treatment as life's crises dictate. Don't accept the guilt trip of someone who says that you shouldn't be in counseling for more than six months or a year or two. Anytime problems seem disruptive to your family and your child, always seek preventive mental health solutions.

Why Start a Parents in Recovery Group?

Self-help groups spring up to meet needs that aren't being met elsewhere in the community. Ever since the enlightened efforts of Bill W. and Doctor Bob culminated in Alchoholics Anonymous, twelve-step programs continue to provide a network of folk wisdom and recovery support. However, the generic recovery group for chemical dependents may be comprised of singles, swingers, seniors, as well as parents. A parent in recovery may be reluctant to deal openly and honestly about his innermost fears and dreads or the seemingly mundane problems of child rearing.

When a parent finally opens up and says, "Sometimes I don't think I can stay with my family and stay sober," he runs the risk of hearing from some well-intentioned but unempathic peer, "So *leave* your family! Your sobriety comes first!" Of course, he didn't really want to leave in the first place. Like Fred in this book, he simply needed a supportive group to listen and help him sort through his feelings of confusion in coping with his family processes.

Or, to the question "How do we go about healing the hurt of our children when we're still struggling to heal ourselves?" who but another recovering *parent* is attuned to the feelings of inadequacy expressed? "So worry about yourself and the rest will follow" might be a typical response from a recovering peer who doesn't see parent-child recovery as a parallel process.

It's true that any recovering parent can go to the group of choice—AA, Al-Anon, NA, CA, or OA—and talk about their problems in parenting. But you may find yourself like the parents in this book, needing and wanting to share with other parents about the *special* problems that you're experiencing with your children.

You may want to join with other parents who respect that you and your children are involved in a *parallel course of recovery*. You'll be encouraged when someone else understands what you mean when you say that *recovery is in and of itself a stressful situation for family life*. You'll want someone to recognize that *your family in recovery is a brand new family as you attempt to organize around the fulcrum of sobriety*. Of course you'll want someone to appreciate and support your efforts as you try to create a better way of life for your child.

We know that supportive recovery networks are crucial in sustaining recovery. Add to that the need for supportive groups to decrease the chances for child abuse and neglect, and you have the need for a Parents in Recovery group.

Many of us are like the parents in this book without extended family support. Our modern age challenges us to adopt new models for filling the needs that were once met by the kinship group or the tribe. The nuclear family of today—many headed by single parents—is already overtaxed and overburdened just meeting the basic demands of life.

Why start a Parents in Recovery group? Decide for yourself whether the recovery of you and your children can be enhanced by such a group. No other healing resource is as effective as you, the parent, in healing the hurt of your children. I am hopeful that many of you will be strengthened in this journey by a twelve-step approach to healing.

Now with all due respect to the original authors of the model for Alcoholics Anonymous, their twelve steps have been adapted for your use in healing the hurt of your children.

Twelve Steps to Healing the Hurt

Step 1: *We admitted that we were powerless over our children's hurt as a result of our chemical dependence and that their lives and ours had become unmanageable.*

As we come to recognize the hurt of our children, *awareness* is the guiding principle. Awareness requires an admission that we have failed, disappointed, and perhaps even abused our children as a result of our chemical dependence.

The second part of the step is meant to help clear the way for a new beginning. When we focus on our children's problems as being "controllable," we tighten the reins of control, and their problems escalate because we have denied their hurt. Feeling more overwhelmed than ever, we will want to run, to flee from the family. When we relinquish control by accepting the "unmanageability" of the parent-child relationship, we can begin to use *awareness* to shift our focus to the child's hurt. This paves the way for healing.

Step 2: *We came to believe that a power greater than ourselves could restore our children's mental health and the parent-child relationship.*

When we come to believe in the need for outside help for our children—for some power greater than ourselves—we can begin to implement a commitment to healing the child's hurt. Whether the power is in a Parents in Recovery support group, a hospital treatment program, a counseling resource, or a spiritual "Higher Power," we begin to help ourselves help our children.

Step 3: We made a decision to turn the life of our child over to the care of the God of our understanding, relying only on knowledge of divine will for our relationship with our child and the power to carry it out.

When we relinquish our child's hurt to the God of our understanding, we are beginning to employ one of the most important principles of healing—faith. This step emphasizes the decision-making process that requires us to begin to see our child as a self that is separate from us. As we "turn the life of our child over," we are not abandoning the child. We are giving up possessive, omnipotent control.

Those of you who stumble over this step because of the notion of God that is implied will be comforted by the emphasis on "the God of our understanding." This God, or Higher Power, can be your self-help group or some other positive recovery resource. I suggest simply throwing an extra "o" into the word, which then becomes *Good*. Who of us would dispute that there is a Good and better way of life for our child?

Step 4: We made a searching and fearless moral inventory of our parenting.

This step stresses a realistic self-appraisal of our parenting. We want to look for those qualities in ourself that we can emphasize and preserve in our parenting relationship. But, as with weeding a garden, we also want to look for areas that have interfered with our previous parenting efforts.

Step 5: We admitted to God, to ourselves, and to another human being the exact nature of our wrongs with our child.

From our previous moral inventory in Step 4, we are now able to *communicate* openly about the specific ways in which we have contributed to the hurt of our children. This step considers the importance of an honest admission to God, to ourselves, and to another human being. The other person may be a counselor, sponsor, member of the clergy, or some other trusted friend in recovery.

Step 6:   *We were entirely ready to have God remove all these defects of character.*

Through the previous two steps, we have come to learn more about the disturbances in our parenting. We are now willing to surrender these to the God of our understanding.

Step 7:   *We humbly asked God to remove our shortcomings.*

This step simply requires us to ask with humility for the removal of our shortcomings in parenting. Again, this is an asking of the Higher Power, the God of our understanding, or the "Good" of our understanding. This step requires faith or the positive conviction that your shortcomings can and will be removed.

Step 8:   *We made a list of the hurts that we had brought to the lives of our children, and we became willing to make amends to them all.*

This step emphasizes the amends-forgiveness process that is so essential to healing the parent-child relationship.

Step 9:   *We made direct amends to our children wherever possible, except when to do so would injure them or others.*

When we accept personal responsibility for our failings, we must carry the amends-forgiveness process forward by acknowledging how we have hurt our children. We must also make it possible for them to be a part of this process by *requesting their forgiveness of us.* We must help free our children of their resentments. This step stresses that we must keep our amends child-centered, framing it in words that will not injure or emotionally overburden the child. Similarly, an amends that is too brief or nonspecific will intensify any hurt that is present.

Step 10:   *We continued to take personal inventory; and when we were wrong in our parenting, we promptly admitted it to ourselves and our children.*

This step emphasizes our need to be actively involved in an ongoing process of preventing further hurt to our children. When we are wrong, we promptly acknowledge that we have failed, hurt, or disappointed. This step recognizes that we are human and imperfect and that we continue to acknowledge that to our children when we are in the wrong. Children are rarely hurt by our mistakes when we offer a sincere apology.

Step 11:   *We sought through prayer and meditation to improve our conscious contact with the God of our understanding, praying only for knowledge of God's will for us and the power to carry that out.*

Because we are human and imperfect, we can actively seek to improve our contact with the God (or "Good") of our understanding through prayer or meditation. This is an exercise in continuing to expand our awareness through faith.

Step 12:   *Having had a spiritual awakening as the result of these steps, we tried to carry this message to other parents in recovery and to practice these principles in all our affairs.*

To extend a helping hand to others is the foundation of all twelve-step programs. When we use the important principles of healing the hurt to restore relationships with our children, we will want to carry this message forward to other parents with a similar need.

The essential difference in a Parents in Recovery self-help group and other twelve-step groups is that we focus not on ourselves but on the hurt of our children. We recognize that to ignore this hurt is to compound it for our child. The escalation of problems in a child can compromise our own recovery efforts.

13 | Epilogue

"Hey, folks, this is a celebration!" Chuck beckoned us to an assortment of sparkling fruit drinks. "Three years ago yesterday we had that first Parents in Recovery meeting. Who'd have dreamed we'd *still* be together?"

"Not me," Betsy said. "I was ready for a divorce."

"But we made it, and our kids did, too. So what better way to celebrate our housewarming than with the people who helped us reunite?"

"Thanks for coming, everyone," Betsy said, toasting with a glass of cranberry-fizz, "and—well, thanks for everything."

"Karra was the one who convinced Bitsy to move," Chuck continued excitedly, "them being best of friends and all. Karra helped Bitsy see that the old neighborhood was going to pot—as in drugs—and that we needed a fresh start with our two youngest."

"I listened to Karra's advice. She knows real estate."

"So after our three oldest moved out, Bitsy and me figured that our family had shrunk down to the size where we could buy our dream home out here in the suburbs."

"A tract home may not be everyone's dream home, but this little place is just perfect for us." Betsy looked proudly over the small, neat living room that still smelled of fresh paint and new carpet.

"Karra got us one heckuva deal. She's as proud of this house as we are. That's why she insisted on giving us the housewarming. Did the whole thing herself from the catering to the invitations."

"Check-out the invitation," Sam said, handing me a neatly printed card. "'You're invited to the OPIRA.' Pretty radical, huh? But if you think that's rad, look at what it says inside:

'Of course Karra can spell opera!
But this is an invitation to the O-PIRA:
Original Parents In Recovery Anonymous
Three Year Reunion.'

Man, talk about corny!" Sam continued. "But it tore at my heart-strings, too. It was so totally *Karra*. I got to missing this old group bad."

"When I first read the invitation, I thought we were being invited to Karra's mansion," Sara said.

"Speaking of Karra," Karra said, entering the room with a large tray of fancy hors d' oeuvres, "consider yourself invited to the mansion for our next reunion. And do bring the kids. They can have a pool party while we're sipping tea in the parlor. But it has to be next year. Otherwise, you may not get to see the mansion. As soon as Angel graduates from high school, I'm out of there!"

"What? The Red Queen without her mansion? You can't be serious," Sara said incredulously.

"I'm putting the whole shabang on the market. Antiques and all. See, I finally got this insight that I'd been trying to live out my mother's life, the way she'd always wanted. I mean, the mansion just isn't *me*. It's who I thought I was. With my lifestyle, all I need is a little self-cleaning condo."

"So you haven't slowed down yet?" Sam asked.

186

"*Slow* and *Karra* just won't fit together in the same sentence," Fred joked.

"Oh yeah? When I don't have to make mansion payments any longer, maybe I'll slow to a snail's pace."

"I'll believe it when I see it," Fred persisted, smiling.

"Look here, old man, you're turning into a regular wit! Has that nonalcoholic bubbly gone to your head?"

"Fred's come out of his shell since he's been chaperoning teen parties. He's loosened up." Mimi beamed.

"Five years of sobriety is what's loosened me—plus a whole lot of meetings with good folks like you."

"Speaking of meetings, we need to put aside the refreshments and have a little refresher course to see how we're applying the principles of Parents in Recovery," Chuck announced. "Can you get us started, Doc?"

"Anyone need a review from the old group or classes?" I began.

"'*Proceed with faith.*' That's what you said at the end of our last class on Healing the Hurt," Fred reminded me.

"You have a keen memory," I said.

"Not really. I can't even remember how long ago the old group ended, but I still hear the echo of your parting words, 'Proceed with faith.'"

"What struck you about those words?"

"Guess my old self-talk had always been 'Proceed with caution' when I was around the kids. I'd keep my distance to play it safe because I didn't know how to be a father. That *faith* word sure has changed things for me."

"How's that?"

"A lot of times when I was trying to be a dad to my kids but didn't know the first thing about what I was doing in recovery, I'd just keep repeating your words, 'Proceed with faith.' That gave me the courage to get in there and try my best."

"When Fred says 'kids,' he's talking about our three daughters: April, May, and June," Mimi clarified, "and, of course, our son, Freddy."

Sam and Sara were laughing and applauding in unison. "Right on, Mimi! Calling your kids by name at last. We're proud of you."

"But you're still playing the role of the good little Co, talking *for* Fred," Sam teased.

"My co-dependence is improved, not *cured*," Mimi said curtly.

"Well, I don't know about the rest of you parents, but I'm still fighting windmills," Karra said, frustration in her voice.

"You mean you feel like a regular Don Quixote fighting that old Recovery Windmill," Mimi observed.

"If you say so."

"When we get caught up in our family processes, we get stuck. Then we can't even reason our way out," Mimi continued.

"We had an example of that last spring when our oldest girl, April, moved into the sorority house," Fred said. "It started with a physical scrambling between May and June, each trying to move into April's bedroom."

"But it was more than that, too. It was about May trying to get the power position that was vacated by April as oldest sister, only June wouldn't allow it. She demanded an equal chance for the bedroom."

"Yeah," Fred agreed, "and then there was this male-female power struggle that got going between Freddy and the girls, and Mimi and I got caught up in it somehow. Freddy was forcing me to his side, the girls had Mimi on theirs, and that got the two of us arguing."

"Freddy was so rude and self-centered—like Fred used to be back when he was drinking—that I just started feeling resentful all over again."

"So I started wanting to run."

"But Fred didn't run. And he didn't drink."

"I kept talking about my frustration at my PIRA meetings until I could get clear on what I needed to do."

"What *did* you do?" Chuck wondered.

"I told Mimi that it was time for us to assert our leadership as parents in the family. Then *we* told the kids that it was our house, so we were going to make the decision about that room assignment. And we'd make it in such a way that each kid got a fair chance for the room."

"Now how did you pull that off?" Karra asked.

"We had them draw straws. Worked like a charm."

"So who got April's room?"

"May. She drew the longest straw. Then June decided that she never really wanted to move in the first place. She likes her room with the special wallpaper. So Freddy moved into May's old room, and everybody is happy. Kids! Who can ever understand them?"

"Fred's become such an effective leader in our family that I actually left him with the children for a couple of months this summer," Mimi said.

"So I got to play single parent for a while. Finally I know what Karra's been talking about all this time."

"Well, PIRA has been helping me help my family keep it together," Karra said. "PIRA meetings *and* continuing to practice that third step about releasing my kids from my own selfish needs to some higher 'Good.' I finally came to see that Billy deserved a relationship with his dad. And so did Angel and Sandy, too, so now they all have visitation on alternate weekends at their dad's place—plus phone calls whenever they want."

"And you're not threatened by that anymore?" Sara asked.

"Threatened? Not really. But the going back and forth between families keeps us revolving like crazy in that old Recovery Windmill. Seems we're always in that stage of Inclusion where the children never know for sure *where* they *belong*."

"Or even *if* they belong," Sam said.

Karra nodded. "But we go through the rough times, and the words I keep remembering from the old group meetings are 'Go with the flow. Don't resist the windmill.' When I feel like I'm losing my grip, I know it's time to loosen up even more."

"I don't get it," Sara looked puzzled.

"Here's an example. A few months ago, the ex called me and asked to have Billy for a couple of months this summer. 'A couple of months! No way! Over my dead body!' I wanted to scream. But instead I held my tongue, and even though I wanted to tighten my grip like a steel claw, I let go. I went to Billy and said, 'Son what do *you* want to do?' I mean, the kid does have a mind of his own, right? Know what he said? 'Sure I'd like to go, Mom, *if* you'll let me come back home after the vacation.' I grabbed the kid and hugged him and kissed him like I'd never done before. I don't think I'd ever felt so close to Billy—or so much at peace about our relationship."

The group was silent as Karra recalled the scene. Brushing tears from her eyes, she turned to Mimi. "Your turn to share about your summer vacation."

"¡Si, como no! I went to Mexico with a couple of other teachers to study Spanish at the University in Guadalajara."

"¡Que bueno! When you go, you really go," Sam said. "Like you're surprised I've got a little Spanish under my belt, too?"

"From his old drug dealing days," Sara confided.

"Speaking of drugs," Sam was quick to change the subject, "whatever came of Buddy's rap for assaulting that girl? Did he do time? Did he get put away? Does he still wear his earring?"

"Hey, thanks for asking, Sam, because I gotta say how proud I am of Buddy. He got through his treatment program for drugs in a little over a year. Then they made him a peer counselor helping these new kids when they first come to the program. Buddy was given one heckuva recommendation from the treatment center by the time of his court sentencing. Then the judge gave him probation."

"Guess he already did his time—in the rehab center," Sam observed.

"Yeah, and then Buddy got himself a scholarship to attend this chemical dependency counseling tract at the university. He'll be a real drug counselor someday. But you're mistaken, Sam. Buddy never wore an earring. That was his younger brother, Charles Junior."

Betsy stirred uneasily. "Wait til you hear about Cassy."

"Who's Cassy?" Sara asked.

"Cassandra, our twin daughter. Oh, I know Chuck used to call her Sassy, especially back when he was drinking. But she's a nursing student now, and she lives with Buddy in his apartment over near the university. They've both been active in twelve-step programs on campus. And last week Cassy and her dad spoke together at a PIRA meeting. They were inspirational."

"We're a father-daughter team at last," Chuck grinned.

"So how about the kid with the earring?" San persisted.

"Charles Junior still wears his earring—though not the same one as before. He's got a fancier one now that he designed himself. It's part silver and — "

"I'm not interested in his earring, man! How's the *kid*!"

"Junior's still shy, not much for girls or speaking at meetings. But he's clean and sober, so I'm mighty proud of him, too."

"Your family is a success story!" Mimi congratulated.

"What's this success jive?" Sam asked with sarcasm in his voice.

"It all depends on how we define success," I responded. "Mental health experts tend to look at our recovering families from different perspectives. Some might count the number of cases of alcoholism and drug abuse in our children, and they would come up with a bleak picture. But to me, the true measure of success in Chuck's case was his family's ability to get into treatment and to stay in programs, continuing the process of recovery, parents and children together."

"We had other problems in our family besides drugs and alcohol,"

Betsy disclosed. "I was an untreated ACoA and a deadly co-dependent. I enabled Chuck and the three older children to drink and use chemicals. I was also a workaholic."

"But Bitsy's been recovering, too," Chuck said. "She got this new job just a few miles from home as office nurse for a plastic surgeon."

"I pushed her into that, too," Karra joked. "I knew I'd eventually need a face lift, and I wanted Bets there to make sure it was done right."

"Bitsy and the doc do some of those cosmetic surgeries right there in the office," Chuck marveled. "I'm proud of this little gal. But the best part of her new job is that she's off nights and weekends."

A round of spontaneous applause broke out in the group.

"Success upon success," Sam said. "This is starting to sound like a Hollywood plot where everything is just one big happy ending. Let's get real, folks! No one lives happily-ever-after in this day and age."

"Like we've still got problems—big time," Sara's voice was unmistakably filled with remorse. "Our Seth kept getting worse instead of better. A couple of months ago he was diagnosed as having this thing called ADD, or Attention Deficit Disorder."

"I know about that condition," Mimi said. "As a fourth grade teacher, I've had a lot of ADD children in my classes."

"Yeah, Seth had school problems, all right, and he was a holy terror at home. I was feeling so desperate I was thinking of sending him back to foster care or somewhere. Anywhere. Not that I'd really do it! But it was getting to me. He was so hyper he reminded me of myself on crystal meth. Wired, y'know?"

"He was a live wire," Sam agreed.

"Some of my ADD students do much better on medication," Mimi said.

"Yeah, Seth's just started meds. This drug called Ritalin. It's a type of speed, but it slows down kids with this condition so they can pay attention and learn." Sara was shaking her head, sadness in her voice. "My kid on chemicals at the age of nine! All of a sudden I started remembering that I was doing speed and coke during my pregnancy with Seth. I'd denied it before. Too much fear to face the truth."

"We were too naive in early recovery," Sam said. "Like we thought our love could cure Seth's problems."

"Love is still the answer," Mimi encouraged. "Perhaps not as a *cure* for alcoholism or any form of addiction or for Seth's condition, but it's definitely what we all need to *heal*."

"And I want to remind Sam and Sara that the whole purpose of PIRA is facing up to our children's hurt and getting them help," Fred said. "We don't even talk about *cures*."

"Level with me, Doc. You wouldn't say Seth is a success story, now would you?" Sam asked.

"Despite Seth's problems, he's being cared for by the two people he needs most in the world, his *parents*."

"So what's that got to do with success?"

"You and Sara have made it possible for Seth to have a course of recovery that runs parallel to your own. He knows that his parents are loving him and supporting him to get the help he needs."

"Love and support from your parents. Guess I forgot how important that is, seeing as how I never had much," Sam said.

"Sam and me have another success story," Sara began tentatively, "if that's what you mean by success. We reunited with *my* folks. So now Seth has a set of grandparents who love and support him, too."

"Tell it like it is, babe," Sam said tensely. "We didn't do the reuniting until they came to make peace with us."

"Yeah, they came all the way downtown looking for us. They'd heard that we were helping street people get off drugs. That qualified us as missionaries in their eyes."

"We level with them that we're recovering addicts, but the only part they let themselves hear is that we're helping others," Sam added.

"So they're still self-righteous—but they adore Seth, and he needs the attention. My folks will babysit anytime they think we're doing our 'missionary work.'"

"Which is more than I can say for my folks," Sam said.

"Still no contact with your family?" I asked Sam.

"My old man could care less about seeing me until I get an M.D. behind my name. Ya know what M.D. stands for? *Mighty Doctor*. You've got to be a cool head to be an M.D., right? I'll never be more than Sam, R.D., Recovering Druggie."

"Proceed with faith, remember?" Fred encouraged. "If you lose faith, Sam, you lose hope. That's when you start to feel like a loser."

"Fred's right. If anyone was ever a *born* loser, it was me," Karra said. "Just think about *my* childhood. It had to be some kind of faith that one day I'd have a mansion that got me through rough times. The *image* of that mansion in my mind and *believing* that one day I *would* have a mansion made it happen. That mansion was *my* Higher Power. But I don't need it anymore since I've found this new Higher 'Good.'"

"Oh, yeah? Like what?" Sara asked.

"Myself. My kids. New beginnings. Today. The miracle of recovery that lets me live life and face myself a little more honestly each day. And, definitely, this group—you people, my dear friends."

"Now that's a positive attitude of faith," Fred commented.

"Oh, I can still bring on an attack of the negatives if I let myself," Karra said, "because my kids still have problems, too."

"New ones or the same ones as before?" Sara wondered.

"Both. Remember Angel, my perfect child, the straight-A student, who had a problem with binge eating? Suddenly, she started getting model trim, about the time that she began weekends with her dad. That was just after she's started high school, too, so I thought she'd outgrown her problem. But, no, she's just become more secretive and learned how to purge."

"So how'd you find out about it?" Sam asked.

"I had a phone call from the mother of Angel's friend. Seems there's a clique of these high school girls that pig-out together, and then they do a group purge—a kind of ritual. I know it sounds disgusting. But she's been on this binge-purge roller coaster all through high school. She has an eating disorder—*big time*, as Sara would say."

"Yeah, I'd say that. Big time problems like that make ours sound trivial. So what're you doing to help the poor kid?"

"I've found a hospital, thanks to Bets, and I'm arranging for Angel to get some intensive treatment," Karra explained.

"We'll help in any way we can," Mimi offered.

"And you can count on us," Sam said.

"Like my folks would probably love to babysit Billy and Sandy with our boy, Seth. Anything to help us 'missionaries', y'know?"

"I'm not sure I'd wish Sandy on your parents," Karra frowned. "She's my problem child these days."

"Never thought I'd hear you say that," Fred said.

"Ever since Sandy started school, I've had constant feedback from her teachers about how immature and demanding she is. I think the word they'd like to use is *brat*. So, I had to face up to my part in spoiling her. I came to see that if she was ever going to change, I had to change. Now I have to show my love in a different way to Sandy by setting firmer limits. This is no picnic, group, but I keep trying."

"You've changed, Karra. You're probably the most changed of all of us," Mimi observed.

"It's your positive attitude of faith," Fred said.

"Hey, Fred and Mimi," Chuck interrupted, "you deserve credit, too, for all you've done to organize our first Parents in Recovery Twelve-step group and keep it going. I'd say you deserve a round of applause!"

Not only did the group applaud, but the members got up in turn to embrace Fred and Mimi, and then each other.

I was deeply touched by this group of people who had become so caring and supportive of each other and of their children. I hadn't seen the members for several years, but I felt a special bond to them. This was a crucial moment for me to share with these parents who had become effective healers of their children's hurt.

There was no better way for me to pay tribute to this group than to bow out quietly. "You're doing great as therapists for your own children and for each other. My job is over, just as it should be, " I said, rising to leave.

"You're going to split?" Sara resisted.

"There's next year's reunion," Chuck reminded.

"You better be there!" Karra urged. "The mansion, remember? Your last chance to see my mansion full of priceless but useless antiques."

"All the kids will be there," Fred emphasized. "You've never even met April, May, and June."

"Or Buddy, Junior, Cassy, Betsy, and Christopher."

"Not to mention Angel, Billy, and Sandy."

"And our boy, Seth."

"Send me an invitation," I said, "and I'll come, but strictly as a guest next time."

"How about as guest of honor?" Mimi proposed.

"As an old friend," I said. "The children will be our guests of honor."

"Hey, how about that?" Chuck was grinning and turning the idea over in his mind. "We'll honor the children as our guests!"

Suggested Readings

The readings I suggested for the members of the Parents in Recovery group are those which I find to be particularly helpful. What helps most is that which rings most true about the subjects of parenting, child development, and chemical dependency.

Cavanaugh, Eunice, M.Ed., M.S.W. *Understanding Shame* (Minneapolis, MN: Johnson Institute, 1989).

Cermak, Timmen L., M.D. *A Time to Heal: The Road to Recovery for Adult Children of Alcoholics* (Los Angeles, CA: Jeremy P. Tarcher, Inc., 1988). Available from the Johnson Institute, 7131 Metro Blvd. #250, Minneapolis, MN 55439.

Cermak, Timmen L., M.D. *Diagnosing and Treating Co-dependence: A Guide for Professionals Who Work with Chemical Dependents, Their Spouses, and Children* (Minneapolis, MN: Johnson Institute, 1986).

Cermak, Timmen L., M.D. *Evaluating and Treating Adult Children of Alcoholics*, Volumes One and Two (Minneapolis, MN: Johnson Institute, 1990).

Faber, Adele and Mazlish, Elaine. *How to Talk So Kids Will Listen and Listen So Kids Will Talk* (New York: Avon Books, 1980).

Faber, Adele and Mazlish, Elaine. *Liberated Parents/Liberated Children* (New York: Avon Books, 1975).

Jesse, Rosalie C. *The Care and Feeding of Children of Alcoholics* (In press).

Jesse, Rosalie C. *Children in Recovery* (New York: W.W. Norton, 1989).

Jesse, Rosalie C. Children of Alcoholics: Their Sibling World. In *Siblings in Therapy*, edited by M. Kahn and K.G. Lewis (New York: W.W. Norton, 1989).

Johnson, Vernon E., D.D. *Everything You Need to Know About Chemical Dependence* (Minneapolis, MN: Johnson Institute, 1990).

Johnson, Vernon E., D.D. *Intervention: How to Help Someone Who Doesn't Want Help* (Minneapolis, MN: Johnson Institute, 1986).

Leite, Evelyn and Espeland, Pamela. *Different Like Me: A Book for Teens Who Worry About Their Parent's Use of Alcohol/Drugs* (Minneapolis, MN: Johnson Institute, 1987).

Schaefer, Dick. Choices and Consequences: *What to Do When a Teenager Uses Alcohol/Drugs, A Step-by-Step System That Really Works* (Minneapolis, MN: Johnson Institute, 1987).

Wilmes, David J. *Parenting for Prevention: How to Raise a Child to Say No to Alcohol/Drugs* (Minneapolis, MN: Johnson Institute, 1988).

References

1. Jesse, R. C. (1989). *Children in recovery.* New York: W.W. Norton.

2. Jesse, R. C. (1989). Children of alcoholics: Their sibling world. In *Siblings in therapy,* M. Kahn & K.G. Lewis (Eds.). New York: W.W. Norton.

3. Whalen, T. (1953). Wives of alcoholics: Four types observed in a family service agency. *Quarterly Studies on Alcohol, 14,* 532-641.

4. Cermak, T. (1986). *Diagnosing and treating co-dependence: A guide for professionals who work with chemical dependents, their spouses, and children.* Minneapolis, MN: Johnson Institute Books.

5. American Psychiatric Association. (1987). *Diagnostic and statistical manual of mental disorders* (Third edition-Revised). Washington, D.C.

6. Jesse, R. C. (1977). *Children of alcoholics: A clinical investigation of family role relationships.* Doctoral Dissertation. California School of Professional Psychology, San Diego.

7. Schutz, W. C. (1967). *Joy: Expanding human awareness.* New York: Grove Press.

8. *Webster's Dictionary of the English Language.* (1988). New York: Lexicon Publications, Inc.

9. Nichols, M. P. (1987). *The self in the system: Expanding the limits of family therapy.* New York: Brunner/Mazel.

10. *Alcoholics Anonymous.* (1976). New York: Alcoholics Anonymous World Services, Inc.

11. Masterson, J. (1985). *The real self.* New York: Brunner/Mazel.

12. Satir, V. (1976). *Making contact.* Berkeley, CA: Celestial Arts.

13. Kritsberg, W. (1985). *The adult children of alcoholics syndrome.* Pompano Beach, FL: Health Communications.

14. Jampolsky, G. (1983). *Teach only love.* New York: Bantam Books.

15. 1 John 4:18. *New American Standard Bible.* (1978). Nashville, TN: Thomas Nelson Publisher.

16. Gibran, K. *The prophet.* New York: Alfred A. Knopf.

17. Sujata. (1983). *Beginning to see.* San Francisco, CA: Apple Pie Books.

18. Kapleau, R. (1980). *Zen: Dawn in the west.* Garden City, NY: Anchor Press/Doubleday.

Index

When the Johnson Institute first opened its doors in 1966, few people knew or believed that alcoholism was a disease. Fewer still thought that anything could be done to help the chemically dependent person other than to wait for him or her to "hit bottom" and then pick up the pieces.

We've spent over twenty years spreading the good news that chemical dependence is a *treatable* disease. Through our publications, films, video and audio cassettes, and our training and consultation services, we've given hope and help to hundreds of thousands of people across the country and around the world. The intervention and treatment methods we've pioneered have restored shattered careers, healed relationships with co-workers and friends, saved lives, and brought families back together.

Today the Johnson Institute is an internationally recognized leader in the field of chemical dependence intervention, treatment, and recovery. Individuals, organizations, and businesses, large and small, rely on us to provide them with the tools they need. Schools, universities, hospitals, treatment centers, and other health care agencies look to us for experience, expertise, innovation, and results. With care, compassion, and commitment, we will continue to reach out to chemically dependent persons, their families, and the professionals who serve them.

To find out more about us, write or call:

7151 Metro Boulevard
Minneapolis, MN 55435
1-800-231-5165
In MN: 1-800-247-0484
or 944-0511
In CAN: 1-800-447-6660

Need a copy for a friend? You may order directly.

Healing the Hurt
Rebuilding Relationships with Your Children
A Self-Help Guide for Parents in Recovery
Rosalie Cruise Jesse, Ph.D.
A Johnson Institute Book
$10.95

Order Form

Please send ____ copy (copies) of **Healing the Hurt.** Price $10.95 per copy. Please add $3.00 shipping for the first book and $1.25 for each additional copy.

Name (please print)

Address

City/State/Zip

Attention

Please note that orders under $75.00 must be prepaid.
If paying by credit card, please complete the following:

☐ Bill the full payment to my credit card.

☐ VISA ☐ MasterCard ☐ American Express

Credit card number: _____

For MasterCard
Write the 4 digits below the account number: _____

Expiration date: _____

Signature on card: _____

Return this order form to: The Johnson Institute
7151 Metro Boulevard
Minneapolis, MN 55439-2122

Ship to (if different from above):

Name

Address

City/State/Zip

For faster service,
call our
Order Department
TOLL-FREE:
1-800-231-5165
In Minnesota call:
1-800-247-0484
or **(612) 944-0511**
In Canada call:
1-800-447-6660